Praise for *Healing Our Future*

"The American healthcare system of the future will be built increasingly on the strengths of teams, not individuals—an environment where everyone will be a leader. *Healing Our Future* will be useful for clinicians and others working in teams, as well as individuals considering the pursuit of their first formal leadership role. The book also contains valuable content and reminders for seasoned executives."
—**Thomas M. Priselac, President and CEO, Cedars-Sinai Health System**

"I have used this amazing leadership model successfully with my leadership team, resulting in a stronger team and excellent individual development and improvement. This comprehensive leadership model will support the success of individual leaders and organizations alike."
—**Cynthia Barginere, COO, Institute for Healthcare Improvement**

"Garman embraces the importance of developing leadership skills in everyone, not just those in leadership positions. He offers a crucial overview of healthcare fundamentals, along with practical guidance and resources. This is a must-have book."
—**Jeanne Armentrout, Executive Vice President and Chief Administrative Officer, Carilion Clinic**

"*Healing Our Future* is a transformative must-read for next-generation healthcare organization and system leaders. Dr. Garman offers a superbly crafted research-based leadership road map, and he delivers it in a clear, accessible, and compelling voice."
—**Annie Tobias, former Vice President, Learning and Engagement, Ontario Hospital Association, Canada**

"*Healing Our Future* is what we need for today and to help us achieve a better tomorrow. The book provides important information in an accessible format that will appeal to leaders at every career stage."
—**Christy Harris Lemak, PhD, FACHE, Chair, Department of Health Services Administration, University of Alabama at Birmingham**

"Sustainable healthcare delivery is a global challenge, and success increasingly requires leadership at all levels. Although written in the US context, *Healing Our Future* offers practical, evidence-based advice that can empower all aspiring leaders to help the health systems they work in to build a healthier future."
—**Ronald Lavater, CEO, International Hospital Federation**

"Leadership is like a fine wine, often taking time and experiences to develop. The development journey in *Healing Our Future* is structured in a way that ensures readers have practical and achievable solutions to evolve their thinking and leadership style, turning challenges into opportunities."

—**Joseph Moscola, Executive Vice President, Enterprise Management, Northwell Health**

"*Healing Our Future* captures the essence of what is required for our leaders as they prepare for the healthcare challenges of the future. The seven disciplines elegantly capture and detail what should be the learning path for our leaders."

—**Chris Newell, Senior Director of Learning and Development, Boston Children's Hospital**

"Andy Garman explores the frailties of healthcare with insight earned from the intellectual rigor of thoughtful research tempered with the scars and bruises from resolute practice. His book presents readers with a blueprint for recognizing their purpose, strengthening competencies, and, lastly but most importantly, being value-driven passionate advocates for health in the community."

—**Anthony Stanowski, President and CEO, Commission on Accreditation of Healthcare Management Education**

Healing Our Future

HEALING OUR FUTURE

LEADERSHIP FOR A

CHANGING HEALTH SYSTEM

ANDREW N. GARMAN

Berrett–Koehler Publishers, Inc.

Berrett-Koehler Publishers, Inc.
1333 Broadway, Suite 1000
Oakland, CA 94612-1921
Tel: (510) 817-2277   Fax: (510) 817-2278   www.bkconnection.com

Ordering Information
Quantity sales. Special discounts are available on quantity purchases by corporations, associations, and others. For details, contact the "Special Sales Department" at the Berrett-Koehler address above.
Individual sales. Berrett-Koehler publications are available through most bookstores. They can also be ordered directly from Berrett-Koehler: Tel: (800) 929-2929; Fax: (802) 864-7626; www.bkconnection.com.
Orders for college textbook / course adoption use. Please contact Berrett-Koehler: Tel: (800) 929-2929; Fax: (802) 864-7626.

Distributed to the U.S. trade and internationally by Penguin Random House Publisher Services.

Berrett-Koehler and the BK logo are registered trademarks of Berrett-Koehler Publishers, Inc.

Printed in the United States of America

Berrett-Koehler books are printed on long-lasting acid-free paper. When it is available, we choose paper that has been manufactured by environmentally responsible processes. These may include using trees grown in sustainable forests, incorporating recycled paper, minimizing chlorine in bleaching, or recycling the energy produced at the paper mill.

Library of Congress Cataloging-in-Publication Data

Names: Garman, Andrew N., author.
Title: Healing our future : leadership for a changing health system / Andrew N. Garman.
Description: First edition. | Oakland : Berrett-Koehler Publishers, [2021] |
    Includes bibliographical references and index.
Identifiers: LCCN 2021012425 | ISBN 9781523090105 (hardcover) |
    ISBN 9781523090112 (adobe pdf) | ISBN 9781523090129 (epub)
Subjects: LCSH: Health services administrators. | Leadership.
Classification: LCC RA971 .G362 2021 | DDC 362.1068—dc23
LC record available at https://lccn.loc.gov/2021012425

First Edition
27 26 25 24 23 22 21   10 9 8 7 6 5 4 3 2 1

Book producer: Westchester Publishing Services
Text designer: Westchester Publishing Services
Cover designer: Adam Johnson
Illustrator: Emily Garman

*To our kids, their generation, and
the next two they will look after*

Contents

Introduction   1

SECTION I   **LEADERSHIP IN THE CHANGING HEALTH SYSTEM**

CHAPTER 1   **The Changing Health System**   7

CHAPTER 2   **Accelerating Your Development as a Leader**   23

SECTION II   **THE SEVEN DISCIPLINES**

CHAPTER 3   **Values**   33

CHAPTER 4   **Health System Literacy**   46

CHAPTER 5   **Self-Development**   70

CHAPTER 6   **Relations**   84

CHAPTER 7   **Execution**   110

CHAPTER 8   **Boundary-Spanning**   122

CHAPTER 9   **Transformation**   135

Conclusion   147

Appendix 1: Developing Mentoring
   Relationships   149
Appendix 2: Developing a Longer-Term Mindset   155
Bibliography   169
Acknowledgments   181
Index   187
About the Author   201

Healing Our Future

Introduction

Every time history repeats itself, the price goes up.
—*Anonymous*

This is a leadership book for people who are more interested in making change happen than in formal leadership roles or titles. In health systems, as in other organizations, leadership has been evolving into a team sport: our environment has simply become too complex to be understood, let alone managed, by a small group at the top of a hierarchy. Regardless of whether "leader" is part of your title, or even in your job description, in the years ahead you will have increasing opportunities to lead. I'd like to help you prepare for these roles as they appear before you, so that you can pursue them with a greater sense of confidence and purpose.

This is also a book about the changing role of health systems in our society. If you are working in a health system, you are working with colleagues who care deeply and inclusively about the health and well-being of others. You are also part of the largest corner of our economy, a sector with both the potential and the responsibility to become a powerful vehicle for pursuing the healthier futures that we know are possible but not certain.

I started my own career as a clinical psychologist, focused mainly on helping individuals in distress find better ways to get their needs met. I did not plan to become a leader, or even to study leadership. Over time, I was doing more and more things that were leadership-like, and then studying leadership to figure out how to do them better. This eventually led to my being asked to run programs, then departments, and then, ultimately, an organization: the National Center for Healthcare Leadership. Over the course of nine years, I had the opportunity to lead numerous research studies examining excellence in healthcare leadership, and analyze the approaches of hundreds of health systems in developing their leaders. The more individuals and organizations I studied, the clearer the commonalities across them became. Cut through all the chaos of personalities and "secret recipes," and every leadership model can be mapped to seven universal disciplines. Similarly, every successful leadership development activity involves a finite set of universal learning principles.

In this book, I provide approaches to help you develop into a more effective leader. I do not assume you are currently in a formal leadership role, or even that you aspire to be—only that you will periodically find yourself with the desire to pursue a greater good in the world, and you will need other people's help along the way. The seven disciplines described in this book form an evidence-based "common language" of leadership—one that you should be able to easily map to any "local language" model your organization or profession may be working with, and in doing so provide a stronger scientific foundation.

The first section begins with a glimpse into our more distant future, and how our health systems could evolve to help us navigate this future more successfully. I then describe how people become more effective leaders over time, and what the research has to say about what works best in making this happen. In section two, I introduce the seven disciplines. The first three—the enabling disciplines—relate to the "inner game" of leadership:

- **Values–** clarifying the greater goods you want to serve.
- **Health system literacy–** understanding how healthcare organizations work.
- **Self-development–** developing and maintaining yourself for success in the challenges leadership often entails.

The next four—the action disciplines—focus on leadership in action:

- **Relations–** understanding and supporting the individual needs of the people you work with.
- **Execution–** clarifying and monitoring the shared direction for action.
- **Boundary-spanning–** managing relationships between your collaborators and the outside world.
- **Transformation–** creating the urgency, vision, and trust needed for more fundamental changes of direction.

Each chapter in the section provides a description of the discipline, illustrates why it is important, and provides specific advice on how to raise your proficiency. In each case, I describe many free and low-cost resources—online articles, videos, and courses—available to help you along the way. I also suggest places you can find good mentors to learn from, as well as additional tools, resources, and background that may be of more specific help, depending on what brought you to this book in the first place. The book concludes with two appendices. The first offers step-by-step advice on recruiting and engaging good mentors. The second provides more in-depth guidance on how to develop your skills in long-term thinking and foresight.

In the coming years, we will likely participate in some of the biggest social changes many of us have seen in our lifetimes. Our health systems stand to play a significant role in the many adaptive changes we need to make to heal our future. I hope you take this book as an invitation to help lead us there.

Leadership in the Changing Health System

B efore diving into the nuts and bolts of effective leadership, I provide some context on why the subject is so important, and how it will become even more so in the years to come. In the first chapter of this section, I share some perspectives on how healthcare is likely to evolve in the decade ahead, based on trends that are already in motion today. With this background, you will be better prepared to identify areas that may be helpful for you to learn more about, and prepare to contribute to. In the second chapter, I summarize the factors that have the greatest influence on how leadership develops over time. With this context, you will be better prepared to put the concepts and recommendations in the later chapters into immediate action.

CHAPTER 1

The Changing Health System

S ay what you will about the year 2020. It was undeniably the gateway to a new decade and a glimpse of the road ahead. It is hard not to equate the whole year with the COVID-19 pandemic, and all of the changes that followed in its wake. For many people working within health systems, these changes meant working under conditions they were never trained for, and learning new skills on the fly. In many cases, it involved developing entirely new approaches to the delivery of care, and learning as quickly as possible from the experiences of peers across the country and the world.

As hard as people worked to mitigate the pandemic, they could only do so much within what their contexts allowed—and that context was a health sector already facing significant challenges. We had just begun to understand the severity of healthcare inequalities when COVID-19 began making them much worse. At a time when we needed resilience more than ever, the sector was already facing problems with clinician burnout and well-being. And our planet's climate, our most important determinant of human health, was about to clock its hottest year on record. COVID-19 did not create these challenges; what it did, more than anything, is reveal how deeply intertwined they are, and how critical it will be to address them simultaneously.

How are our health systems likely to continue evolving in the decades to come? The answer depends partly on trends taking place outside these organizations' direct control, and partly on how well we understand these trends and the opportunities they can create.

In a recent foresight study for the National Center for Health-care Leadership, our research team identified four macro-level trends that are particularly likely to shape the future of health-care and have specific implications for leadership within our health systems. All of this work took place before the onset of the COVID-19 pandemic and the civil unrest that reemerged in its wake. It even predated the climate strikes Greta Thunberg led. None of these events were predicted by our modeling, and no one expected them to be. They are the types of emergent events that, in the moment, can seem quite random. Events of this type—sudden, unexpected, dramatic—can lead people to feel very powerless about the future. Attempting to predict a specific event or a specific timeline not only is impossible but also misses the real value of foresight work. The futurist Bob Johansen (2017) makes this point very well in distinguishing *certainty*, an assumption that we know what is coming, from *clarity*, a deeper sense of multiple potential future states, some more likely than others.

For example, although no one predicted a novel coronavirus would begin to spread among humans in late 2019, many public health experts had said they believed a pandemic was likely to happen sometime during their lifetimes. (One of the most colorful and compelling examples was Bill Gates's excellent TED talk from 2015: "The next outbreak? We're not ready." Worth a watch if you haven't seen it.) And although no one could have predicted beforehand that the events surrounding George Floyd, Breonna Taylor, Ahmaud Arbery, and others would galvanize action the way that they did, understanding the underlying forces at work—heightening awareness of racism within the context of growing structural inequality—makes clear their eventual inevitability.

Forces such as the cyclical nature of human social and economic history, the patterns through which new technologies find acceptance and are spread, the influences of demography, and the root causes of attraction and disgust each offer specific clues about the robust trends and the interplays between them, providing greater clarity about these longer-term trends. With practice, these trends can be analyzed to develop a clearer sense of the directions the future is likely to take us, and the inflection points that decide which paths will prevail. For the interested reader, I provide greater detail on sources of data and foresight methods in appendix 2. In the meantime, the four trends we identified for health system leadership in the decade to come are given below. As you look at these health system trends, I invite you to consider whether the events of 2020 truly changed their course, or just accelerated us toward them.

Trend #1: From Expertise to Relationships

If you have ever taken a course on research methods, or conducted some research yourself, you may have run across the idea that good experiments often raise more questions than they answer. As health professions mature, the volume of research relevant to their work also tends to grow very rapidly, quickly outpacing the capacity of practitioners to keep up. Although technologies such as better search tools can assist caregivers in identifying the most important studies related to specific health problems, we only have so much time in a day we can spend in search of better methods. This can result in very long delays—decades, according to some research—before research advances become standard clinical practice (Morris, Wooding, and Grant 2011).

In the realm of accessing and organizing information, computers have some important advantages over humans. For one, they can process text more efficiently and more rapidly. For another, their "memories" (information storage) are much more reliable. They also do not get tired. I could list more advantages, but at some point it starts to get a bit demoralizing. The main point is that the use of computer-assisted tools in healthcare has been growing, helping care providers become more effective in their roles.

Good news so far, right? There's just one hitch: if care providers can access these decision-support tools, what stops the patients they serve from *also* accessing them? And if my patients can access these same tools, what do they need me for?

With telehealth quickly becoming more prevalent, clinicians' roles may evolve in some unexpected ways. As more patients begin accessing care through video connections, it is not hard to imagine a pathway toward lower-cost care providers. The first wave could involve price shopping in a patient's local community. That could be followed by price shopping in different communities or worldwide. And once we are conditioned to getting our care through a computer screen, could software-controlled, animated chatbots of some kind be that far off?

These are, by the way, just the sorts of threats that professional associations were set up to grapple with. If you pay dues to such an association, it's a safe bet that it would like you to continue doing so. The best way for associations to do that is to make sure your professional status isn't threatened. So they may attempt to block direct consumer access to these tools. Based on prior playbooks, arguments will likely revolve around safety and will contain enough of a grain of truth that they cannot be completely dismissed. On this basis, they may be successful in slowing progress by years, if not decades.

But progress will come all the same. How can I be sure? Two reasons. The first is simple economics. Selling goods and services directly to consumers is usually more lucrative, because doing so cuts out the expensive "middle man" in the form of the health-care professional. The second is human nature. Throughout most of our history, when we were sick, we did not seek out the expertise of a stranger in a strange clinic; we instead looked to ourselves and our loved ones for care that was delivered in our own homes (Lilly, Laporte, and Coyte 2007). Over-the-counter medications provide a handy example. Many of these medications, such as Claritin and Tylenol, originally required a prescription, meaning you could take them only while under a providing doctor's supervision. Once they became over-the-counter, however, most people had little concern about self-diagnosing and self-administering, or even having them on hand for family members in need.

Does this mean the roles of professional caregivers are going away? Hardly. If anything, they are likely to expand. To see why, let's think again about the historical model of caregiving, the one that existed before experts were around. In that model, the fundamental ingredient was not expertise but rather a trusting, caring, and understanding relationship. And when it comes to our health, most people are not going to completely trust what they learn from their loved ones, or the internet. But before you breathe a sigh of relief, it is important to consider what this means. Although the need for the health professions is not going away, it is likely to fundamentally change. While *technical* expertise may not distinguish care providers the way it once did, *relationship* expertise will become far more important. Keep this in mind when you read the chapters on self-development and relations.

Trend #2: Expanding Roles in Adaptive Change

While a proper discussion of the history of the U.S. healthcare system is far beyond the scope of this section, a few key points are in order. First, healthcare costs are a barrier to a great many people receiving proper care, and costs are continuing to go up. I'm guessing this may not be news to you. Second, in the United States, this cost trend has been identified as a "massive crisis" since at least 1969 (Millenson 2018). Since that time, much effort has gone into "bending the cost curve"—in other words, slowing and stopping the escalation of costs. And yet, the costs keep rising. Why? One reason has to do with inertia. As I will expand on further in the chapter on health system literacy, growth is the path of least resistance for our current economic systems, and health systems are fundamentally economic systems. Shrinking, or even staying the same size, is much more difficult than continuing to grow. Another reason has to do with a health system's core "products": life and health, which, among mortals anyway, are in constant, insatiable demand.

Over time, many health systems have grown very large and sophisticated. The largest ones often have their own training departments and conference spaces. Some have extensive campuses—miniature cities, with retail shops and other extensions of the health system's "brand." In the United States, health systems have already become the largest employer, and by 2028 they are projected to represent almost one in every five dollars that get spent (Keehan 2020). Alongside this tremendous growth, health systems are also increasingly struggling with an existential problem: How can they continue to justify their need for escalating costs in the absence of equally escalating outcomes?

The most promising way to address that problem is through expansion of mandate. As communities become more concerned about the health and well-being of their citizens, health systems will find themselves taking increasingly active roles in helping their communities holistically pursue these goals.

I want to underscore that this is an *expansion* of mandate, not a new one. Throughout the history of modern medicine, many people working in healthcare voluntarily pursued a whole host of community activities beyond the scope of their formal clinical professions, including education, research, and advocacy. What has started to change, and will look different in the future, is the extent to which these activities become organized and formally "blessed" by the organizations we work for. In the United States, we began to see the beginnings of this formalization in 2012. It came as part of the Affordable Care Act (or "Obamacare," as it is often called). Although the act is mostly known for its focus on getting more people insured, it also contained a number of important new expectations for the health systems. One of these expectations was that they complete a periodic Community Health Needs Assessment (CHNA), a systematic, comprehensive data collection and analysis to identify priority health needs and issues in the communities they serve. Another was that they use the results of the CHNA to formulate a Community Health Improvement Plan (CHIP), spelling out what they plan to do about the health gaps identified by the CHNA. Collecting data about communities wasn't a new activity for the health systems. Most had already been doing this for years. What changed was the focus. Historically, most data collection related to healthcare needs—for example, how many people were likely to need hip or knee replacements in a given year, and how that number was likely to change over time. The data were primarily to inform plans for growing and marketing healthcare services. What changed with the CHNA and CHIP was a broadening beyond the delivery of healthcare services, and toward improving *health*.

At Rush University Medical Center, where I work, this early CHNA activity included examining the average life expectancy of people living in different neighborhoods on Chicago's west side. The results were alarming: in neighborhoods close enough to walk between, average life expectancies differed by as much as 12 years (Rush University Medical Center 2016). Some neighborhoods had life expectancies that rivaled the healthiest countries in the world; others were similar to the least healthy. The findings had an immediate and profound impact on the organization's leaders, raising fundamental questions about how the health system was approaching its work. In the words of Dr. Larry Goodman, CEO at the time: *"With these kinds of data, how do you justify your mission statement without committing to a solution?"* (Goodman, personal communication with the author, February 17, 2017). Across the country, many progressive health system leaders were beginning to ask the same question. In searching for an answer, some of these leaders began thinking differently about the economic power their health systems represented.

The *anchor institutions* concept offered an intriguing starting point. In the context of economic development, an *anchor* is an organization of substantial size that is deeply rooted in the community where it is located, and whose success is intertwined with the community's. Arguably, these types of organizations—nonprofits, in particular—have both the opportunity and the responsibility to support the vitality of their home communities. While the anchor institutions idea has been around since at least 2002, its original focus was mainly on the roles universities should play in their home communities (Initiative for a Competitive Inner City 2002). Over time, it was becoming clear that the same logic could be applied to health systems, and with much greater potential impact.

To better understand the anchor institution concept, it is helpful to work through an example with a fictional hospital. First we need a name. How about we call it . . . wait for it . . . Fictional Hospital, or FH for short. (Hey, it's a better name than Fictional Health. Think about it.) Let's say FH earned $153 million in revenue, which was roughly the average for U.S. hospitals back in 2011 (Becker's, n.d.). In a typical year, after all expenses, FH might clear about 2 percent of that amount as net revenue, or $3 million. So what should FH do with all that money?

One option FH leadership has, in theory anyway, is to ignore any internal needs of the organization and instead invest the whole amount in community health improvement programs. That $3 million could do a lot of good in the community. However, it is a much smaller amount than the $153 million that the hospital originally took in. Yes, the hospital has to pay its bills, but, wow, if any of that other 98 percent of revenue could somehow be routed toward community health, FH could potentially have a much, *much* bigger impact.

So let's take a closer look at FH's expenses. Using national averages again, a typical hospital of FH's size would spend about $30–$45 million on "procurement": products and services needed to keep the place running. Some of this expense may be for high-tech equipment that has to be imported from other places, because maybe no one in the neighborhood has figured out how to slap together a good MRI scanner or robotic surgery machine in their garage. But there may be other expenses that could have stayed local with a little more effort. Laundry services is a good example. Some hospitals send their dirty linens out of town, not because there are no closer options but because options that are farther away are a lot cheaper. If hospital leaders are focused only on efficiency, such decisions make sense. If, however, the leaders are considering community impact in addition to efficiency, their decisions may change. In this case, stable employment is itself an important source of health, so there are important health-related reasons to encourage creation of local jobs.

Do I sound like I may be going off the rails here? It's one thing to talk about hospitals buying locally, but I just kind of implied that FH ought to consider investing in commercial laundromats. And that's just one example. There are lots of other causes of health problems that might also make for good investments from a health perspective. How about all the people who don't have ready access to fresh fruits and vegetables? Should hospitals start opening up grocery stores? What about homelessness? Should hospitals invest in low-income housing? Even if this makes sense philosophically, where on earth would they find the money?

As it turns out, most hospitals in the United States actually have sizable stockpiles of cash. They need to, in fact, in order to be eligible for loans with favorable interest rates—something most hospitals must access regularly. One of the benchmarks creditors use for good financial health is having "200 days' cash on hand," meaning enough accessible funds to be able to cover the costs of running an organization for 200 days straight without any other income. If it costs $150 million per year to run a hospital, 200 days' cash on hand works out to a nest egg of about $82 million, another much bigger number than the $3 million we were talking about originally. Realistically, it would never make sense for hospital leaders to blow this whole nest egg on a bunch of potentially risky investments in laundromats, grocery stores, and apartment buildings. Chances are, they already have the money invested in much safer places. But it could make sense to move at least a few million into investments that can pay health as well as financial dividends—something some health systems have already begun to do.

This brings us to the last, and most sizable, resource FH can use to impact the communities it serves: its payroll. The single biggest expense most hospitals have is personnel, which accounts for 55 percent of total expenditures (Daly 2019). For an organization the size of FH, this could amount to $82 million *per year*. Like many other hospitals, FH may also be the largest employer in its community. From a health perspective, many healthcare jobs offer important advantages over jobs in other sectors. For one, they are often more stable, and job security is known to be important to health. Many jobs within healthcare also pay higher-than-average wages. Even for healthcare jobs that may not pay as well, FH could help employees find their way to higher-paying jobs by supporting education and career-pathing programs. These types of programs require additional expenditures outside of the direct payroll costs, but they also produce gains in the form of decreased recruiting and new hire costs, as well as grateful employees.

To the extent that gains from career-focused learning programs outweigh their costs, they are more accurately described as investments rather than expenses. Returns on investment increase when the up-front costs can be decreased, and increase further still if the costs are covered by someone else entirely. Support for these types of programs from outside may become all the more common in the future, for reasons related to our next trend.

Trend #3: Communities Becoming "Service Lines"

Clinicians and the health systems supporting them tend to be very serious about care quality and work continually on improving it. However, when it comes to people's health, there is only so much a health system can do through the care it provides. In reality, only about 10–20 percent of people's health relates to the quality of healthcare they receive (Hood et al. 2016). The rest relates mainly to a set of factors collectively known as the social determinants of health (SDOH).

At their essence, SDOH refer to differences in living conditions that impact health outcomes. They include factors such as the level and quality of education a person receives, the quality of food and water they have access to, the amount and security of income they collect, the safety of their work and living places, and the extent to which they perceive they have equal rights (World Health Organization 2020). The work that health systems have engaged in around SDOH, at least so far in their history, has been supported mainly through either voluntary activities or funds generated from their core business: clinical care. But as prior trends illustrated, we are beginning to wake up to just how complex some of our social challenges are, and how much coordinated effort they will require to solve.

What do successful coordination efforts look like? Answers to this question are crucial to the work of organizations like the Federal Reserve Bank of San Francisco and the Low Income Investment Fund, whose roles involve investing in efforts to solve community challenges. These two organizations conducted an extensive review culminating in the 2012 book *Investing in What Works for America's Communities*. In summarizing across their findings, they drew three key conclusions (Erikson, Galloway, and Cytron 2012). First, new approaches need to be entrepreneurial as well as fundamentally cross sectional, drawing in and engaging many more collaborators than have historically been involved in community development. Second, the approaches need to be evidence based—that is, highly data driven, allowing for ongoing course adjustments based on what the data reveal along the way. Third, they require a focus on both people and places. The report also identified the need for a new player in community development: an organization that could integrate participants and resources across the full spectrum of communities, including organizations focused on education, housing, community empowerment, and health. They called this new entity the "quarterback organization."

Although their summary did not suggest where these new quarterback organizations would come from, in many ways the role seems natural—indeed, almost inevitable—for our health systems to take. For one, the sheer scale and complexity of health systems mean their leaders need to be effective coalition builders across many competing interests. The services that health systems provide tend to be very data driven and data responsive, involving ongoing adjustments to activity based on data related to volume, quality, patient experiences, and other sources. Also, although historically the health systems' focus has tilted very strongly toward people and not places, their growing responsibility for the overall health of populations is pushing them toward developing place expertise as well. Finally, as noted previously, health systems are under increasing pressure to justify both their current size and their continued growth. Taking a leadership role in addressing seemingly intractable community problems is about as compelling a justification as I think anyone could come up with.

This leadership role will only become more complex, and more important, as we begin adapting to changes in our most fundamental determinant of human health: the earth's climate. In the years ahead, scientists anticipate we will continue trending toward more extreme weather, greater challenges to food and water supplies, and much greater numbers of climate refugees, all of which are ongoing threats to community health and well-being (Watts et al. 2021). Healthcare professionals will be increasingly called on to help advocate for greater attention to carbon emissions; and, to become credible leaders, they will first need to make sure their own houses are in order. Healthcare lags many other industries in its attention to carbon emissions and is substantially more energy intensive than most other commercial activities (Salas et al. 2020). Over time, almost every aspect of how health systems currently operate may need to be reviewed in light of its carbon emissions impact. Through this lens, the sheer magnitude of health systems' economic power may indeed have the potential to shift the broader economy in the directions needed.

Taken together, these trends could lead health systems to look and act very different than they do today, from the services they provide, to how they think about patients, to the boundaries of the organization itself. Our final trend speaks to this evolution of the organization at an even more fundamental level.

Trend #4: People as the Common Denominator

What is a "health system"? I have used the term many times already without bothering to define it. If I asked people working in healthcare this question, the answer might be something like "a group of hospitals and clinics that are all part of the same corporate structure." I think that is a reasonable definition. Now I will ask a harder question: Who, exactly, makes up that health system? The first pass at an answer generally focuses on employees: people who are paid by the corporate entity for the services they render. If pressed, we may need to broaden the definition to include volunteers: people who are formally recognized as supporting the organization in some specific way, regardless of whether they are paid to do so.

Now, let's flip the question on its head and ask, Who does a health system serve? Patients (or consumers or customers)—in other words, the people who pay the health system in exchange for some form of care—may immediately come to mind. Here, too, the need for a broader definition quickly becomes apparent:

if a health system provides care for someone who has no means to pay for it, we would of course still argue that the health system is serving them. So perhaps receiving care is enough to be considered a patient or customer.

If you agree with all the above, then you agree that a person can be considered part of the health system as long as they are working to support its mission, and you also agree that a person is served by the health system as long as said health system is trying to improve their health. This essentially means that any patient of the health system who takes a role in managing their own health is also part of the health system. It additionally means that anyone whose work for the health system benefits their own health is also someone the health system is serving. In the end, the system and the served are more like two different perspectives rather than two truly distinct phenomena.

If there is little real distinction between employees and patients, why do we think about them so differently? The answer relates back to the healthcare professions and the unique expertise they bring to their caregiver roles. If I am sick and you have something that can help me get well, then we have the basis for a transaction, although not necessarily an equal one. Structurally, the caregiver has the upper hand. Think about it this way: If I as a patient walk away from the transaction, the provider could lose a little bit of income. I, on the other hand, could lose my health—or even my life.

As we discussed in trend #1, the power differential between patients and providers has been diminishing, and while I may never be the best person to cater to all my own health needs, my choices for who I seek care from have been expanding. Trends #2 and #3 are also very relevant here. As health systems find themselves more involved in community health, the role of the workplace becomes all the more salient. If the average person spends a third of their life at work, it stands to reason that what happens there—what they eat, how active they are, their sense of accomplishment, and the quality of their relationships—will account for a third or more of their health outcomes. In other words, the work itself must become a critically important piece of any health system's efforts to improve well-being.

Patient, employee, community member: the distinctions are more about the perspective we are using to organize our thinking than actual, concrete distinctions in the world around us. If they clarify expectations for us in specific interchanges, they can be helpful. But if they create enduring power imbalances, they may cause more harm than good.

The same principle is true about hierarchies within organizations. As the patterns of change in the external environment continue to become more complex, top-down leadership structures have more trouble adapting to them successfully. The organizations that thrive will have more egalitarian structures, where people have the skills as well as the flexibility to enter and exit leadership roles more fluidly based on current and emergent needs. In other words, leadership will be viewed less as a job of the few, and more as a role we all need to take when circumstances require it.

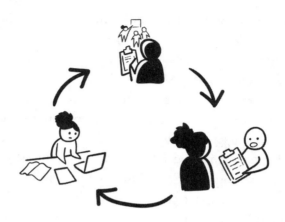

CHAPTER 2

Accelerating Your Development as a Leader

Before diving into the disciplines of effective leadership, it's important to have some context about the leadership learning process. In this chapter, I will describe what we know about how people end up in leadership roles, and why—and, once they are in them, how they become more proficient over time. Here and throughout this book, my focus is on leadership roles in the broadest sense, not just formal leadership positions specifically.

How Someone Becomes a Leader

At its most fundamental, *becoming* a leader involves just two steps. The first step involves acting the part of a leader. The second step

involves other people recognizing what is happening and agreeing to play along. It really is that simple. To understand why *doing*
leadership can be so hard, we need to explore two follow-up questions: Why would you want to lead? And what makes you more
likely to be followed?

Why Would You Want to Lead?

The most important reason to decide to lead is because there is
something you want to see happen that you are not able to do
by yourself. Maybe you love your job, but the clinic you work in
is dark and dreary and you want to fix this. Maybe you notice
some patients having a lot of difficulty getting to your clinic—or
picking up prescriptions, or keeping them refrigerated, or any of
a whole host of other barriers to their care—and you want to find
ways to make it easier for them. Perhaps you are troubled that
no one in your organization seems to give much thought to recycling, or the energy being squandered on excess air condition-
ing, or whether it's really necessary for every single employee to
come into the office every single day. You could always ask your
boss if she could do something about it. If she cares about the
issue as much as you do, and she doesn't already have enough to
worry about, maybe she will. But if you instead offered to pursue a solution yourself, she may very well prefer that you have a
go at it. If so, then congratulations. You now have yourself a leadership role, and all associated opportunities and expectations.
Now all you need is for everyone else to go along with the idea.
Succeed at that, and you're golden. But if you don't succeed, well,
then you're no longer really leading.

Enough with the hypotheticals! I want you to think about a
specific goal or vision that you may already be leading people
toward, or—even better—one that you would be interested in leading in the near future. A realistic example is best: ideally, a vision you already care deeply about, and a role that can be readily

arranged (e.g., starting a new special interest group, leading an improvement effort of some kind, or recruiting a group of volunteers to participate in a community service project). This step is important for applying the next set of ideas. Ready? OK, we can now consider either why people are already following you or why they should be.

What Makes a Leader More Likely to Be Followed?

When you decide to follow a leader's agenda, you are agreeing to give something up in the process. For one, you are putting some level of trust in that leader. You are also agreeing to prioritize working on the leader's interests over at least some other ways you may have spent your time. Why would you, or anyone else, agree to that? The answer generally falls somewhere on the continuum between *because I want to* and *because I have to*. Want-to reasons include (1) a shared set of values around the leader's goals, (2) a belief (based on past successes) that the leader is capable of accomplishing these goals, (3) a sense that the leader is interested not just in the shared goals but also in your welfare, and (4) a conviction that the leader can be trusted to be true to her word. Have-to reasons, in contrast, include things like (1) I must go along with the leader in order to meet my personal goals (e.g., being recognized as a team player, getting a salary increase, having the favor returned one day), and (2) if I do not go along with this leader, I am putting myself at risk (e.g., looking bad or losing my job). Want-to and have-to judgments are very individualized; they will look different for each leader-follower relationship. Although both the want-to and the have-to reasons can work for you, as a leader your best bet is to line up as many want-to reasons for each of the people following you as you can. When you run out of those, that's when you may need to reach for your have-to reasons.

You are striking me as a quick study. Or maybe this stuff really isn't as complicated as I seem to want to make it. In either case, we are now ready to look at how people get better at leading over time.

How Leaders Become More Effective over Time

The fastest path to more effective leadership is similar to the path toward proficiency for most other disciplines. It involves repeating the following three steps: (1) practice, (2) feedback, and (3) reflection, in preparation for . . . wait for it . . . more practice. The differences between leadership and other disciplines mainly relate to the types of practice, feedback, and reflection/preparation that are most useful. Let's consider each.

Practice

Earlier in this chapter, I asked you to think about a specific goal or vision that you would like to lead people toward. Well, given how important practice is, part of me thinks I should just tell you to stop reading this book right now and go do that thing you thought up. Since I'm not the kind of person who likes to order people around, I instead want to point out something very important to your development as a leader: if you *do* go after that leadership role you thought of, it will almost certainly make you a better leader than if you do not.

The research on the role of practice in proficiency is remarkably clear, dating back many decades. One particularly influential study, published in 1993, examined the extent to which practice and innate talent work together in virtuoso musicians. Before this research was conducted, the conventional thinking of the time was that musical talent was something some were born with, and others were not. In their systematic study, the researchers found that innate ability actually mattered very little, and amount of practice was what really made all the difference (Ericsson, Krampe, and Tesch-Romer 1993). The authors then took the findings and applied them to other domains of expertise, such as chess, gymnastics, tennis, and swimming. Everywhere they looked, the same pattern of practice over talent emerged.

The study is as remarkable for its findings as it is for its original purpose, which was to call into question the persistent and centuries-old idea of "innate ability," a genetically transmitted predisposition to excel in a particular area. It was a belief that could be used to encourage some people to pursue a passion, and convince others that they were wasting their time. The field of leadership research shares this difficult past, in the form of debates around leaders being "born" or "made." Yes, history has at times supplied us with templates for what a prototypical leader "should" look like, but these have been based on convention, not performance. The reality is that effective leaders are either made or not made—the difference depends on whether they pursue leadership roles, and how successfully they learn from the roles they occupy.

The amount of practice you get in leadership roles makes a big difference in your effectiveness. So does your approach to the practice you are getting. If you are simply repeating an activity without much thought, you are getting lower-quality practice. Higher-quality practice (also called *deliberate* practice) involves intentionally focusing on improving specific aspects of performance. Since leadership is an interpersonal activity, focus alone won't get you there: you will need feedback from the people you are working with.

Feedback

In leadership roles, getting good feedback can be really tricky. Let me illustrate why with a couple of quick thought experiments. First, have you ever made a judgment about the quality of someone else's work? Of course you have. We make these evaluations all the time. But for most of us, we make far more judgments about others than we share with them. Critiquing a leader can feel risky, especially if the leader is your boss. Most of us are judicious in how often we share our critiques, even if we think they could help a person. Why risk ruffling feathers?

Second, have you ever asked for honest feedback from a friend or colleague, but all they tell you is something like, "You did great!" There isn't a lot you can do with that kind of feedback, other than perhaps enjoy a vague sense of self-confidence, if you thought the feedback was genuine. Even when asked for, people's feedback may not be very useful unless they have clear guidance on what you are looking for. Let's take the example of professional presentations. If I am in the audience of a presentation and the speaker later asks me, "How did I do?" I may think he is asking me for emotional support or reassurance rather than genuine feedback. In this case, if I say "You did great!" I think I am giving him what he wants. But even if I think he is asking for a critique, I may not have a very clear sense of what he is most interested in. Is he hoping to strengthen the quality of his arguments? The strength of his voice? The appropriateness of his attire? As we will discuss further in the "Relations" chapter, giving *more* feedback isn't necessarily a more generous approach. At a certain point critiques can become overwhelming and actually undermine performance improvement if they challenge one's self-confidence too much. But imagine if instead of asking, "How did I do?" after the fact, the speaker instead approached me beforehand with the following request:

> Andy, I have a favor to ask. I know you have a lot of experience presenting, and people think really highly of your skills. I am working hard at improving my own skills in that area, and I'd be grateful if you could give me some feedback on how I am doing—maybe right after my pre-

sentation this afternoon, if you can spare a few minutes. While I'm interested in any tips or advice you may have, there are two areas I'd especially like feedback on. One is eye contact. I have been told in the past that I look at my notes too much, and I need to work on connecting with each person in the audience. The other is standing relatively still and not fidgeting. Would you be willing to do that?

First of all, if I don't get compliments like that very often (and I assure you I do not), there's a good chance this person just made my day. I am going to find it very hard to say no to such a seemingly small ask from someone who is putting so much effort into buttering me up. More importantly, he has just given me very clear instructions on exactly what he is looking for. I am now well primed to monitor the specific things he is most interested in, and give him very targeted and useful feedback about those areas. With this higher-value feedback, he will learn much more from the practice than he otherwise could have. This brings us to the next step in the learning cycle: reflection and preparation.

Reflection and Preparation

Feedback is only useful if it can enhance the approach we take to future work. Feedback that we ignore, forget, or give too little thought to will have much less impact than feedback that we take to heart, analyze, and use in planning for next time. While this may seem a rather obvious point, getting the most out of the feedback you receive is itself an important skill. Research on leadership development, as well as on performance improvement more generally, offers several useful suggestions. The first is to set specific goals around what you are looking to improve. (The chapter on execution provides additional guidance on how to structure goals for maximum impact.) The second is to commit to your goals in front of someone else—an *accountability partner* (Harkin et al. 2016).

Your Own Leadership Development

The next section of this book describes the seven disciplines most closely associated with effective leadership for the greater good. Each chapter is structured to help ensure you can apply the guidelines from the current chapter to the discipline at hand. Every discipline is further divided into several competencies, providing more specific behavioral descriptions to help articulate what effective performance looks like. The end of each chapter has a section with specific recommendations you can apply to your own development. "Learning through Experience" suggests work and voluntary assignments that offer particularly valuable opportunities to practice these disciplines, followed by "Mentors and Role Models," which offers tips on where to find people who are likely to be good sources of expertise. I end each chapter with "Resources for Learning More": articles, books, videos, and courses for readers interested in taking a deeper dive. There I emphasize resources you can access at very little or no cost, ones that I have direct experience with or that other colleagues working in healthcare have told me they found very helpful.

The Seven Disciplines

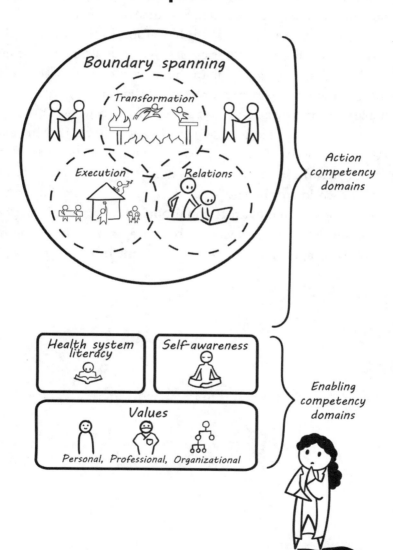

I n the chapters of this section, I will introduce you to the seven primary disciplines associated with effective leadership. Each discipline is based on an extensive review of published research on leadership effectiveness, supplemented by primary-source studies conducted in collaboration with the National Center for Healthcare Leadership (Garman, Standish, and Wainio 2020). In working with these disciplines, I have found it helpful to split them into two broad categories: *action* and *enabling.* The *action* disciplines describe leadership in the context of getting the work done: setting and resetting direction, collaborating inside and outside your organization, anticipating what's coming, and helping people prepare for it. The *enabling* disciplines, in contrast, involve "offline" work that makes leadership efforts more effective: learning more about yourself, deepening your understanding of the world around you, and taking care of yourself. Because the enabling disciplines are foundational to success in the action disciplines, we will start with these concepts, beginning at the base of the diagram with *values* and working our way up.

CHAPTER 3

Values

U nderstanding the true nature of the leadership role requires a clear understanding of values. The basic concept of *values* involves beliefs about what is most important. Values are a critical ingredient for most of our decision-making, big and small. For example, think of the last food you ate: How did you decide what to eat, and who to eat with? If you prioritize long-term health over living in the moment, you may have chosen carrot sticks rather than curly fries. If you value your personal space, you may have eaten alone; but if you place greater value on being with others, maybe you found company. Of course, values help us with much weightier problems as well. In this chapter we will consider three sources of values that are particularly relevant to leadership: personal, professional, and organizational. We will also look at how these sources of values can come into conflict, and how our approaches to resolving these conflicts influence how people judge our effectiveness as leaders.

Personal Values

Personal values are the most central to your sense of who you are as an individual. They are shaped by your experiences growing up, especially by your primary caregivers as well as any other people who had a lot of influence over your life. At their core, personal values provide guidance about the most complex and difficult of life's problems, including the meaning of our lives in the face of our inevitable mortality.

Yes, mortality. Of all the awful and scary things we as humans have come up with to worry about, our mortality continues to top the list. Once you figure out you are going to die, it's something you can't unknow. The best approach we have found for coping with this reality is to find meaning in the life we have and, through this meaning, come to terms with its ending.

The many religions of the world have served this purpose quite well throughout most of recorded history. A central value shared by almost all of them is serving a "greater good"—the less fortunate, or people in general, or life and nature itself. Unfortunately, religion can also fall prey to a basic human tendency to sort people into in-groups and out-groups. In these cases, people who don't follow a particular religious doctrine can feel like a direct threat to the whole point of the doctrine in the first place: finding meaning in the dark space of our mortality.

Social scientists came up with the name terror management theory to describe this phenomenon (Greenberg, Pyszczynski, and Solomon 1986) and have been studying its effects for decades. This body of work has described, in great detail, how remarkably hardwired we seem to be to fear our own mortality, and how motivated we are to manage these fears through the construction of meaning. It has also found that we are hardwired to feel very threatened by personal beliefs and values that we view to be incompatible with our own (Burke, Martens, and Faucher 2010). It turns out that accepting differences in others' beliefs does not come naturally to us: it may instead be something we need to work on actively throughout our lives (Solomon, Greenberg, and Pyszszynski 2015). Thankfully, we also tend to be quite good at keeping these kinds of concerns out of our thoughts most of the time. This allows us to interact and collaborate with people without worrying about how our personal values may differ. Many of us are conditioned early on to avoid these topics altogether, unless we are with people who already agree with us.

Personal values also influence the career path people choose. In some cases, a person's career path may be chosen—or at least heavily influenced—by a family member or caregiver. Going along with the choice is still an exercise of personal values, although it is a different kind of pathway. It can cause other challenges down the road, especially if the chosen profession is not a great fit for the individual's other personal values.

Professional Values

Before discussing professional values, we first need a clear definition of what a profession is. A good place to start is with the idea that a "professional" is someone who is paid for their work. We can quickly make things more complicated by asking whether you would be considered a professional care provider if you were, say, twelve years old and your neighbor offered to pay you a few dollars to watch her kids. A more restrictive definition might also require some level of skill, demonstrated prior success, or both. Tightening up the definition further, we might focus on work most people do not know how to do themselves and could not learn to do quickly. In other words, they would need to complete a course of study of some kind and then demonstrate specific competencies. This leads inevitably to another thorny question. If a so-called professional knows more than you do, then by definition it would be difficult for you to judge whether they are actually competent. So how could you ever completely trust such a person?

The description I just went through illustrates four common elements identified by many definitions of professions: (1) application of a specific and complex set of competencies, (2) agreed-upon educational pathways through which these competencies are developed, (3) a set of ethical principles that identify the profession's responsibility to society, and (4) a means through which the profession as a whole can, on an ongoing basis, ensure its members practice competently and ethically (Bowen 1955; Peterson 1976). Professional values are most closely tied to the third component, relating to the purpose of the profession within broader society. While values differ from profession to profession, some of these distinctions are based more on differences in language than actual differences in the values themselves. Three value sets, in particular, appear to be shared across nearly all healthcare professions: altruism (compassion, caring, empathy), equality (human dignity, respect, social justice), and capability (excellence, competency, knowledge) (Moyo et al. 2016). These three values also tend to apply to the health systems within which these professions come together.

Organizational Values

As with people and professions, organizations also have their own values, as well as their own belief systems. These beliefs describe why the organization exists, what it hopes to accomplish, and how its members should approach their work. Within health systems, these values are frequently encoded as a set of five to seven words or short phrases, often assembled into an easy-to-remember acronym. They may also be formulated into a set of explicit ethical standards, or behavioral descriptions. They are often taught to new employees as part of an initial orientation process and may feature prominently in employee recognition programs.

When taking on a leadership role, organizational values can be an important resource for your work—especially if senior leaders are themselves using the values in their own communications, which will suggest they take them seriously. If you spend the time to frame a shared goal in terms of organizational values, you will put yourself, and others working with you, in the best position to justify why the work is important and why it should be prioritized. We will return to this idea in the chapters on execution and transformation; for now, I mainly want to underscore why this framing can be so important.

Priorities and Trade-offs: "Competing Values"

When researchers look at how patterns of values transcend individuals, professions, and organizations, they often find it helpful to frame them in terms of a set of trade-offs (see figure 3.1). Although there are many models of what these trade-offs look like, in my experience they differ more in the nuances they focus on rather than their basic architecture. Usually these trade-offs are represented as two axes. One axis relates the *what*: valuing an internal focus versus valuing an external focus. The other relates to the *how*: valuing existing rules and conventions versus valuing flexibility and individual discretion.

Trade-offs along these dimensions seem to show up regardless of whether researchers are looking at individual and professional values or organization-level values (Cameron and Quinn 2011; Schwartz 1992). When looking at individuals, the trade-off

3.1 Competing values

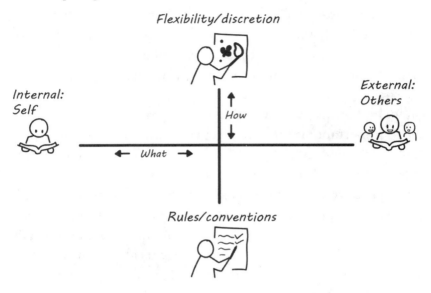

between the internal and the external reflects the extent to which someone prioritizes self-development (e.g., through practice, study, or seeking influence) or service to others (e.g., through clinical service, mentoring, volunteering). At the organization level, the trade-off is between focusing on building and evolving the organization (e.g., building staff morale, career opportunities) and responding to the external environment (e.g., surveying customers, responding to regulatory changes, monitoring competitors).

Individuals, professions, and organizations also differ in the extent to which they emphasize existing standards versus trying new things, to some degree reflecting their relative age and maturity. When a profession is newer, there may be less experience and science to draw on for guidance, so more of the work needs to be guided by an individual's experience and discretion. However, as more collective experience is gained as to what works, there will be less perceived advantage—and greater perceived risk—in ignoring a proven strategy on the chance that an un-proven one may perform better.

These two axes can be particularly useful in thinking about balance: no individual, profession, or organization can thrive if it stays too far to the extreme on either of the two axes, and often we can be farther in one direction than may be ideal for what we are trying to accomplish. For example, rules and conventions, which can be an important source of security, can feel less professionally fulfilling, because they provide fewer opportunities to exercise individual judgment. Conversely, while having all of our decisions completely under our control would maximize our sense of autonomy, having full responsibility for every action and decision can also feel overwhelming, to the point that people find they are overthinking their actions. Similarly, too much emphasis on personal goals, while perhaps materially enriching, can leave people feeling empty because it does not provide an adequate sense of connection to a higher purpose. Conversely, while service to others tends to be far more emotionally rewarding, it can also leave people feeling burned out if they aren't adequately attending to their own needs. Identifying these types of imbalances—through surveys or group discussions, for example—can help start a productive conversation about how to move to a better balance.

Values in the Leadership Role

Leadership roles typically require working with people to balance their competing interests and managing the values conflicts they represent. Success in managing these conflicts in others begins with successfully understanding and managing your own internal ones. To understand this process of growth a bit better, I will build a bit further on ideas from chapter 1 about developing as a leader.

In the first leadership role any of us takes, we have no direct experience to draw on. All we have is whatever worked for us in any prior attempts to influence people. Maybe you have received a little advice from experienced leaders, but for the most part, your best first guide is your accumulated experiences of trying to get other people to go along with some idea or plan you had. For example, if you are the oldest sibling in a big family, you may have learned to use your size and strength to compel your younger siblings along. If you were a youngest sibling, you may have learned to observe the mistakes your older siblings made in trying to get things done, or used your parents' protectiveness to your advantage. In the process, you may have learned that parents and other authority figures could be helpful, or maybe that they were not to be trusted. In any case, these prior experiences will form the starting point for your initial approach to leadership.

As you try out these old methods and receive feedback on them, you will find that some of them still work well and others do not. Over time, you will try new approaches to see if they work better. Between these experiments and the feedback you get, a new style of interaction will begin to take shape. On the left side of figure 3.2, the little bump in the upper right depicts this development. Your approach to leadership is still based mostly on your life experiences, but you are starting to develop an approach

3.2 Leadership maturity

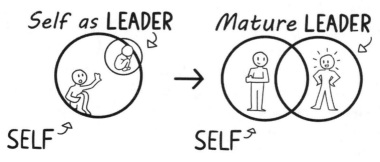

to leadership as its own new activity. Over time, as your experiences and successes grow, so too does the leadership "bump." The illustration to the right of figure 3.2 depicts this matured leadership style. More of the leadership role sits outside your sense of yourself now, but it still shares a healthy amount of connection to who you are and what you value.

This healthy equilibrium is not always so readily achieved. The two illustrations in figure 3.3 depict imbalances between the self and the leader roles. In the illustration on the right, the *overinvolved leader*, the leader role is not distinct enough from the self role. In this case, the person may be taking the leadership role much too personally. Leadership can involve a whole host of activities that may cause frustration, disappointment, or outrage in other people. It is important to be able to listen openly to that kind of feedback while also keeping it at a healthy distance from your sense of who you are. If a person has too much of their sense of self-worth tied up in their success as a leader, this kind of feedback can feel devastating. Leaders who are described as defensive, having a short fuse, or being unable to accept criticism without lashing out may have *overinvolvement* with their leadership role.

Problems can also occur if a person does not take full responsibility for their leadership role, instead downplaying it or claiming "I'm just following orders." The *underinvolved leader* illustration in figure 3.3 depicts this lack of connection between the self and the leadership role. I often see this happen when someone is first promoted into a manager role and now needs to change the nature of their relationships with their coworkers. This new manager can no longer just be an advocate for her peers; she also needs to be an advocate for the organization they all work for. She needs to become a translator between her staff and the organization, resolving conflicts and pursuing harmony as best she can.

For example, let's say a staff person has made a request for a piece of equipment, and the request gets denied. An *underinvolved*

3.3 Leadership imbalances

leader might say something to him like "If it were up to me, I'd have approved the request. But the guys upstairs said no" and just leave it at that. At best, this communication will leave the staff person thinking that organizational leadership doesn't care about him; at worst, he might become suspicious of whether the leader had actually put much effort into getting it approved. Had the leader taken a more balanced approach in the communication, she might instead have explained the reasoning behind the denial, and perhaps coached him on how to strengthen the argument for his request in the future.

Having a better understanding of how the system works will not only put you in a better position to work within it but also help you identify the ways it could be made better, and how to advocate for its evolution. In the next chapter, "Health System Literacy," I will provide a closer look at what makes our health systems tick, and describe how you can use this knowledge to lead with greater impact.

Strengthening Values: Learning through Experience

Unlike the other leadership disciplines, values are less a skill that you develop and more an understanding that you clarify. You can begin to develop a better understanding of your own values by more mindfully and intentionally reflecting on the decisions you make, taking note of choices that seem to go against what you believe to be your core values. Pay special attention to any decisions where you feel guided more by the demands of your job or other roles than by what you believe is right or best: these disconnects may suggest limitations of the system you are part of, and ways to influence or reshape it from the roles you currently occupy.

Approaches to gaining a deeper understanding of professional values will depend on the nature of your work, or, if you are a student, the kind of work you are preparing to pursue. If you are a practicing clinician, there are likely to be professional associations creating a collective voice on behalf of your profession. If there is more than one association serving your profession, I recommend taking a close look at the values statements of each, and how they differ. In addition to profession-specific associations, there are also many values-focused associations, where membership is more about a specific mission than a professional background. You can find more examples on almost any topic by doing an internet search combining your values of interest along with the phrase "professional association."

Mentors and Role Models

You can learn a lot about values and values conflicts through conversations with people who are willing to reflect on their own experiences with you. Values become most apparent when they come into conflict—for example, when a personal goal collides with a professional one, or a professional goal with an organizational one. Asking experienced colleagues about the most difficult professional decisions they have needed to make will often point to values conflicts, which are often then clarified in the course of their resolution.

Asking more experienced colleagues about their histories with professional associations can also be very illuminating, particularly if you are in the process of making a membership decision yourself. Good questions include: Why did you decide to join? How long have you been a member? What are the ways you use your membership? What do you like about the organization? What do you find lacking? These are also good questions to ask of any current member of an association you may be considering joining.

Resources for Learning More
The personal values matrix I described earlier is most authoritatively described by the work of Shalom Schwartz (2012), who has made an in-depth discussion of his frameworks available for free online. Validated surveys have been developed using this model, which are also freely available for your use and exploration (Gosling 2020). In terms of professional values, resources will depend on which profession(s) you align with, but I can generally recommend the most relevant association websites as a good starting point. I also encourage you to develop a deeper understanding of the role of professions in society generally, both their benefits and their problems. The Center for the Study of Ethics in the Professions at the Illinois Institute of Technology hosts many resources on these topics, including a searchable ethics code collection spanning over 4,000 codes and guidelines extending over 40 years (www.ethicscodecollection.org). Finally, if you are interested in learning more about how professions' roles in society may evolve in the years to come, I recommend Daniel and Richard Susskind's book, *The Future of the Professions: How Technology Will Transform the Work of Human Experts* (Susskind and Susskind 2015).

At the organization level, many collaborative efforts have formed around causes that health systems and other organ-

izations are better able to address collaboratively than individu-
ally. I describe several of these in the chapter on boundary-spanning.
Participating in collaboratives can help organizations learn more
rapidly from one another, as well as accelerate progress by agreeing to publicly visible challenge goals. The presence of meaningful goals can also help you distinguish between collaboratives
that are worth participating in because they are likely to effect
true change.

CHAPTER 4

Health System Literacy

What cruel mistakes are sometimes made by benevolent
men and women in matters of business about which they
know nothing and think they know a great deal.
—*Florence Nightingale*

Health systems, like all organizations, bring together a set
of resources in the service of a specific mission and vision.
How resources get used depends partly on prevailing laws, partly
on history and convention, partly on longer-term planning cycles, and partly on immediate necessity. The more you understand these opportunities and constraints, the better able you
will be to lead effectively within the context of your own health
system. In this chapter, we will consider how health systems manage each of the three primary resources they work with: finance
(money), human resources (people), and information systems

(any and all kinds of data, including information about money and people).

Finance: How Organizations Earn and Manage Their Money

Many healthcare professionals would rather not think about, let alone talk about, the financial side of their work. Yet financial resources are critical for effectively supporting any organization's mission of healthcare. With very few exceptions, organizations need money to survive. This also means organizations need plans for finding money reliably and ensuring that the money on hand doesn't run out before the new money shows up. Getting this right, and doing so consistently, is critical—keeping in mind, again, that we are talking about an organization's survival.

In the next few pages I will introduce two particularly important cycles related to finance: the revenue cycle and the budget cycle. For the revenue cycle, I trace an example of some money flowing into a healthcare organization to illustrate where it comes from, where it goes, and who deals with it along the way. I will try to provide just enough detail to give you a basic sense of financial management systems, and, hopefully, an interest in learning more. (Said differently, I am hoping to keep things unrealistically basic so that the example doesn't become unbearably dull.) We'll use Linda for our example, and I'll set this up like a word problem with some questions to noodle on as we go.

Revenue Cycle

Linda wants to come in to a local clinic because she has been having trouble sleeping. She makes her appointment for the following Monday and will be one of 100 appointments the clinic attempts to squeeze in that day. During her appointment, she spends about 10 minutes with Fred, the front desk clerk, who collects some information from her and checks on her insurance coverage. Linda then spends about 15 minutes with Nate, the nurse practitioner, who gives her several behavior and dietary recommendations to try in the coming weeks. She thanks Nate for his time and gets up to leave, a little disappointed that she wasn't offered a prescription for the sleeping pills her aunt takes, but also relieved that she has some new approaches she can try. On her way out, Fred tells Linda that the appointment will cost a total of $50. Linda writes a check for $10 (her co-pay), and Fred sends a bill to her insurance company for the other $40.

The first question is, How much money does the clinic now have? Unless you are already an expert in finance, your answer may have been guided mainly by your personality. If you are an optimist, you may have guessed $50, meaning you assumed that the bills the clinic sent and the check Linda wrote are as good as money in the bank. If you are more of a pessimist, you may have instead guessed $0, recognizing that neither the bill nor the check is the same as having actual cash. Bills and checks are really more like promises, ones that will hopefully be kept, but occasionally will not. If all goes well, the clinic will indeed receive $50. Eventually. And, hopefully, before the clinic already ends up owing that $50 to someone else.

This description provides a glimpse of the *revenue cycle*, the administrative and clinical functions supporting the capture, management, and collection of money that is owed to an organization. The big goal of managing a revenue cycle is to keep it running as quickly and efficiently as possible, while at the same time making the experience as hassle-free as possible for people receiving care. This is much, much easier said than done! I will illustrate a little bit of the complexity as we look at examples of major phases of revenue cycle management. Here I say "examples" because there is no single, universally recognized set of steps in revenue cycle management. Organizations differ in how they

4.1 Revenue cycle

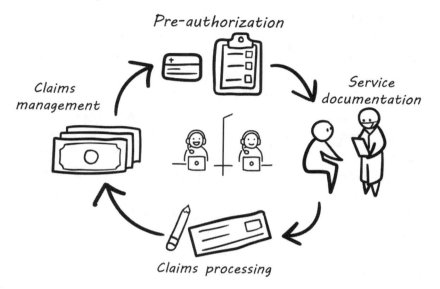

break the steps down: some describe it based more on internal processes, whereas others describe it based on a patient's experiences. Most descriptions I have seen involve between four and eight stages. Being a fan of simplicity, I will use four.

The first stage, is *pre-authorization* (see figure 4.1). During this step, a patient's identity and any sources of insurance coverage are verified. In Linda's example, she may or may not have insurance. If she does, the insurance plan may or may not recognize the clinic she chose as part of its network, which will determine whether the clinic is even eligible for reimbursement from the insurer. If the clinic is recognized, the services she is seeking may or may not be covered, and if they are, the reimbursement rates may differ from one insurance carrier to another based on prior negotiations. The second stage is *service documentation*. During this step, care providers create a record of the services Linda received. This documentation, along with the eligibility and reimbursement information, is then pulled together during stage three: *claims processing*, which essentially means preparing and sending out bills for services rendered.

As noted previously, just because a clinic sends someone a bill doesn't necessarily mean it will be paid in a timely fashion, or even paid at all. The purpose of the fourth stage, *claims management*, is to oversee the process of collecting as much of the revenue the clinic has earned as is feasible. For example, if the 100 patients who visited the clinic that Monday were a representative group from across the United States, about 16 of them would have a past-due medical bill (Batty, Gibbs, and Ippolito 2018). Also, if care and insurance were a similarly representative group, about 19 of the claims sent to insurers would be denied payment (Pollitz, Cox, and Fehr 2019). For these cases, our example clinic can't simply say, "Oh well, we tried." It needs to attempt to get some of these bills paid. Some of these collection efforts may involve negotiating with insurers; others may involve working with patients to create manageable payment plans. In some cases, overdue bills may be "sold" to an organization that specializes in collecting unpaid bills, in exchange for a portion of the bill's value. The clinic may also decide that some services should simply be written off as a loss, as part of its service mission. However the proportion of bills written off needs to be managed very carefully, to ensure the organization has the funds it needs to pay its own bills.

All of this activity requires quite a bit of time and effort—and expense. Health systems in the United States need to spend a lot more on managing the revenue cycle than do those in other countries, and it is one of the reasons healthcare in the United States costs so much more than it does in countries with simpler payment systems (Himmelstein, Campbell, and Woolhandler 2020). At the organization level, changes in insurer agreements can cause big swings in the overall revenue of health systems, as can delays in payments. These risks need to be factored into a health system's ongoing strategic management. This brings us to a second very important financial cycle: the *budget cycle*.

Budget Cycle

For an organization to survive, its leaders need to make sure that it has more revenue coming in than expenses going out. They also need to make sure the revenue arrives in time to pay the expenses, or at least they need a plan in case they need more time. The budget cycle is the means through which this process is organized and monitored.

Although modern-day budgeting looks different than it did hundreds of years ago, the cyclical nature still ties back to an era when a lot of the economy was tied to annual growing seasons. To this day, our economic systems continue to revolve around a 12-month period. The same is true for organizations, which organize their financial accounting and reporting around a *fiscal year*. The timing of the fiscal year typically relates to whatever makes the most sense in terms of the annual cycle of the organization's activity. In some organizations, the fiscal year is the same as a calendar year: it starts January 1 and ends December 31. In other organizations, like many universities, the fiscal year begins July 1 and ends June 30. Regardless of the specific period, every 12 months organizations are required to provide an accounting of how things have been going for them financially. Many larger organizations are also required to arrange for an annual *audit*, an independent review of their finances, which helps ensure that what they are reporting is accurate.

While timing and specifics vary quite a bit from organization to organization, a workable general description of budget cycles can be created by separating activities into four quarters, each lasting three months. (To my earlier point about our agricultural roots, there are also four seasons in the year.) In the first quarter, illustrated at the top of figure 4.2, finance leaders will have

4.2 Budget cycle

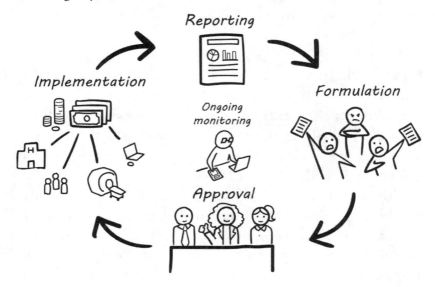

a greater focus on *reporting*, taking stock of the prior year and preparing reports for review by auditors and other outside groups. After these steps, they will shift their focus to budget *formulation*, planning the budget for the next fiscal year. In a large organization, this process will begin with the board and/or senior leadership, who will consider the longer-term financial needs of the organization, in addition to ongoing operational needs. Many larger expenses (buildings and information systems, for example, as well as interest on loans) need to be planned for well in advance and need to relate broadly to the entire organization. Leaders also need to make sure that revenues will be sufficient to meet these longer-term needs.

Once high-level goals for revenues and expenses have been set, they may then be divided into financial expectations for the divisions or departments constituting the organization. Departmental leaders will then build out a budget that they think can meet these goals. In some departments, the goals will seem unrealistic, and there will then be some back-and-forth negotiation to land, hopefully, at something more mutually agreeable.

As you might imagine, this process can get pretty contentious. Since organizational leaders are held strictly accountable for living within their budgets, no leader will want to submit a budget that they believe is going to be extremely difficult to meet. So there is a bias toward asking for too much rather than too little. Additionally, leaders who have been through the budgeting process a few times (also known as having "been around the block") may anticipate they will be asked to improve on an initial budget they submit, no matter how reasonable it was in original form. In these cases, they may pad their initial budget with unnecessary expenses so that it is easier to reduce the budget in later rounds. To help counter some of these tendencies, organizations will often develop philosophies and guidelines designed to help ensure that decisions are made based on the best interests of the organization's mission, rather than its cleverest negotiators. One common approach is to look at how other organizations staff different departments and services, and use these outside examples to provide benchmarks as to what may be most fair.

Once the organization is through this iterative process, the next stage is *approval*. Every organization has a governing body that is ultimately responsible for its oversight. In nonprofit health systems, this body is often referred to as the board of trustees or board of directors. (In my generic example I am describing this step as taking place during quarter 3, but different organizations will use different timelines.) Once approved, the organization's leaders are ready for *implementation*, turning the new budget into the plan at the start of the following fiscal year.

Financial performance is also monitored throughout the year, and actual financial performance will be compared against the budget on a quarterly or monthly basis. This ongoing monitoring allows health system leadership to both more swiftly address financial shortfalls and more quickly add support in areas that are growing faster than expected. Other unexpected opportunities and needs can also evolve across the organization throughout the year. To manage these changes on an ongoing basis, organizations will have approval processes employees can use to get emerging requests considered. How an approval process works will typically depend on how big of a variation from the budget the request represents, as well as the length of the financial commitment. Small-scale requests (e.g., replacing a broken workstation) may be managed at the department level; larger and longer-term requests (e.g., signing a property lease) may require approval at a higher level. Requests to create new positions typically fall into the latter category, for reasons I will discuss further in the next section. First, though, I want to offer some strategic advice about the budgetary approval process that may be helpful regardless of your current role.

If you work within an organization and, like most people, you do not have a budget that you are personally in charge of, you will need to get a manager's approval in order for the organization to make a purchase on your behalf. Depending on the nature of the expense, your department may already have a budget set aside that could cover the cost. Office supplies are a good example: many departments budget for these based on the prior year's expenses, so if the need for your request is clear and the cost is not too high, it may be easy for your manager to approve your request. But now let's say the cost is more significant—for example, a new software application or a new computer or attendance at a conference. These types of expenses are usually best planned for as part of an annual budget, but they can of course still come up as emergent needs or opportunities.

How might you get such an expense approved off cycle? Your success will likely depend on how strong an argument you can make that the expense, as well as its timing, clearly benefits the organization at a level that exceeds the expense itself. There are two primary ways to successfully make this argument. One is economic: the expense will either lead to additional revenue or offset other expenses. The other is mission: the expense will move the organization's agenda forward in ways that clearly justify the cost. Of the two, the stronger case is almost always made by explaining how the expense more than pays for itself.

Framing expenses in this way is a very useful habit to develop, even if you work in a setting where you aren't regularly asked for these justifications. For example, say you are struggling with old software or an old piece of computer equipment. If you can temporarily access a newer version, you can estimate how much quicker this version can make your work. If you have a computer that crashes periodically, you could estimate the number of hours you are at less than full productivity for a given period of time, and then extrapolate it to a full year. The estimates do not need to be perfect; they just need to be a defensible attempt to quantify the value of the expense. This same approach applies to expanding staff. If the team you work on collectively spends 40 hours a week on activity that someone else could do at a lower cost, freeing your team to spend that time on higher-value work for the organization, you are on your way to making the case for an additional staff member.

Human Resource Management: How Organizations Manage Their People

Human resources (sometimes called employees, associates, team members, or people who get a paycheck from the organization) are the single biggest expense in most health systems. It costs a lot of money to find people, persuade them to come work with you, ensure they are doing their best work, and keep them from leaving. For an organization to run as efficiently as possible, all of these activities need to be managed as efficiently as possible.

As with finance, the activities of human resource management can also be usefully described in terms of repeating cycles. One of these cycles is also annual and may include, for example, benefits plan changes (sometimes called "open enrollment"), health screenings, completion of mandatory trainings, employee engagement surveys, performance appraisals, and pay increases. As with fiscal years, the timing of these elements can differ quite a bit from organization to organization.

Another important cycle, one in which I will go into a bit more depth, is the *employment life cycle*. Unlike the annual cycles described previously, the employment life cycle is continuous, with different employees occupying different phases of the cycle at different times. Functions within HR are often organized around these specific phases of employment. Here again, specific labels and stages differ from organization to organization, in this case using between four and eight components. In figure 4.3 I illustrate the life cycle using four stages, with a fifth function (planning and monitoring) tying the rest together.

The first of these stages is *attracting and recruiting*, also known as *talent acquisition*. In larger organizations, this function may fall within its own department. The team making up this department may be responsible for cultivating the organization's reputation as a great place to work, either directly or in collaboration with other departments such as marketing and/or public relations. For some organizations, these activities may include entering "best places to work" contests and pursuing other relevant types of employer certifications and designations. They may also involve sending recruiters to job fairs at universities and community hiring events to build awareness about the organization and the kinds of jobs it offers. The success of these efforts is of-

4.3 Employment life cycle

ten gauged using metrics like the number of hits on the organization's jobs/careers website, the average number of people who apply for open positions, and the proportion of desirable candidates who accept offers of employment.

The second stage, *hiring and onboarding*, focuses on specific open positions and the people being hired to fill them. Consider our earlier case example of Linda visiting the clinic and the two people she interacted with: Nate the nurse practitioner and Fred of the front desk. Before Nate and Fred were on the scene, these were two open positions, and a hiring manager went through a formal process to decide the two of them were the right people for these roles. The clinic then needed to make a job offer to each of them. How would the clinic know how much of a salary to offer Nate? Or Fred, for that matter?

These kinds of decisions need to be made based on several guiding principles. An important driver, always, is efficiency. Keeping in mind that the largest expense most health systems have is their people, HR leaders generally need to set salaries that are high enough to attract people to the job, but not so high that the organization is spending more than it needs to keep them from leaving. Such decisions are typically informed by looking at comparative data about what other employers are paying people in comparable jobs. Since it is generally illegal for companies to share their pay practices directly with each other, this information is usually compiled by independent companies that share the data as industry averages.

Another very important consideration is fairness. Imagine you have been working at the front desk of another clinic in the health system for the past several years, and you have been a dedicated staff person and hard worker all of that time. You then meet Fred at a company picnic, and you learn he was recently hired right out of school, with less experience than you had, and is being paid several dollars an hour more than you are for almost the exact same work. You would probably think this is rather unfair, and you may get pretty upset about it. This reaction is so universal that there are numerous employment laws designed to prevent this unfairness from happening in the first place, especially to people who have historically tended to get a worse deal in the workplace. Organizations need to be careful to stay on the right side of these laws, or they will risk being sued. Since lawsuits are the kind of thing that can cost a lot of money for very little benefit, organizations are generally highly motivated to avoid them.

Organizational leaders also need to look outside to determine competitiveness of compensation. Imagine if the clinic that eventually hired Fred had instead offered him a salary similar to yours. You may have felt that was fairer, but what if Fred had turned the offer down for another job that offered him more? Paying lower salaries only saves an organization money if people are willing to accept them. If no one accepts a salary offer—or if they leave soon afterward for more money—then the clinic can't run, which means it can't make any money, and any potential savings becomes a moot point. For this reason, managers typically need to pay attention to what other organizations pay similar staff, and make sure that their salary offers are competitive. As noted earlier, there are companies out there that collect this kind of information and sell it to other companies so that they can set fair market rates for their salaries. In the case of hiring Fred, the organization may need to set a higher salary to address competitiveness, and then raise the salaries of its current front desk clerks to address this fairness issue. Given the amount of time and effort associated with all of the above monitoring and analysis, these and related functions are typically centralized in an HR department with a name like *compensation and benefits* or *total rewards*.

The third stage, *engaging and developing*, focuses on helping current employees do their best work. While a lot of this responsibility rests with employees' direct managers, larger organizations usually seek to support their managers through a central department with a name like employee and organization development. The work of this department may include, for example, providing learning programs for employees who have been identified as having leadership potential, creating career pathways to help employees pursue higher-paying jobs in the organization, monitoring and addressing staff learning needs, and surveying staff about their perceptions of the organization's leaders. The performance of this department may be measured through employee engagement surveys as well as success in staff retention (or, said differently, keeping staff turnover low). Both areas are particularly important to organizational effectiveness. Staff retention has a direct benefit, in the form of higher productivity (Shanafelt, Goh, and Sinsky 2017) and lower costs associated with recruiting and agency staff. More engaged employees are also significantly less likely to leave the organization (Collini, Guidroz, and Perez 2013) and more likely to provide greater "discretionary effort," voluntary effort contributed to a job beyond what is minimally necessary (Shuck 2011).

The fourth stage, *transitioning*, involves moving people out of their positions. As long as we all remain mortal, no one will stay with a job forever. Assuming good health and good performance, some people may retire out of their positions. Others may leave their positions for personal reasons. In some cases, a person may not be performing well enough, or consistently enough, for their manager to have confidence the organization is getting what it is paying for. Alternatively, an employee may have done something that violates company policy or may make work very difficult or unenjoyable for their coworkers.

Job transitions represent another source of risk for organizations, especially when they involve removing someone from a position. If the affected employee is part of a labor union, her interests may be represented to the organization's management by a union steward. In larger organizations, there may be an entire department devoted just to working through these types of difficulties. Often these departments go by names like employee and labor relations. The success of these departments may be measured by the amount and types of litigation they manage, and the rate at which they prevent complaints from turning into lawsuits.

In addition to the four stages I just described, most HR departments have an ongoing focus on *planning and monitoring*. Because staff are both the most pivotal and the most costly resource a health system needs to manage, organizations need to continually keep tabs on how effectively all activities in the life cycle are being managed. In larger organizations, there are staff or even entire departments dedicated to managing the collection, analysis, and reporting of human resource data. These individuals or departments may go by names like people analytics, talent insights, workforce planning, or some combination of these terms. Sophisticated people analytics departments may include interdisciplinary teams of industrial psychologists and data scientists, who look for patterns that can help identify management development needs, predict turnover risks, and uncover other potential sources of organizational inefficiency. Pursued in the right ways, these types of activities can quickly cover their costs by reducing sources of personnel inefficiency throughout the organization.

At this point, if you went into your line of work because you just wanted to help patients, you may be looking at all of this additional activity and wondering if there isn't a better way. For example, couldn't a lot of these non-patient-facing activities be automated somehow? Turning back to our clinic example, maybe we do need Nate, who is a caregiver, but couldn't Fred be replaced by a kiosk of some kind? You don't have to recruit kiosks, or pay them a specific market rate, or analyze their risk of turnover. Wouldn't this be better? The answer is a definite "maybe." Or an even more definite "sometimes." To look a little deeper at this question, we now turn to our third major area within health system literacy: information systems.

Information Systems: How Organizations Manage Their Data

Information systems are an organization's methods for collecting, storing, processing, and distributing data. The processing step is why they are called information systems rather than data systems: data become information when organized in ways that carry meaning (for humans). For our purposes, *all* organizational data—whether about patients, employees, supply stocks, the organization itself, or the relationships between them—are relevant to information systems.

Good information systems have the potential to help organizations run more reliably and more efficiently. They also typically require substantial financial investments, and it can take a long time before their benefits exceed the up-front costs. Worse still, the estimates of cost savings made at the time of investment are often overly optimistic. Electronic health records (EHRs) are a noteworthy example. In 2005, before most health systems had them, an influential independent study suggested they could save the U.S. health system upward of $81 billion a year (Hillestad et al. 2005). The study was very influential in moving legislation forward to encourage widespread adoption of EHRs across the country. Unfortunately, the results did not live up to these initial expectations. One national study of U.S. hospitals found no evidence of cost savings at all, even after five years of adoption (Agha 2014); another study, this one involving community practices, found they had each *lost* an average of $44,000 per physician during the first five years of investment (Adler-Milstein, Green, and Bates 2013).

The cautionary tale here is not about the value of information systems per se, but whether they represent a significant return on investment. Although health systems spend far less on information systems than they do on people, they still end up costing a lot—more than three cents of every dollar these organizations spend, by one estimate (HIMSS 2014). For an average-sized U.S. hospital, this can amount to millions of dollars every year. Information systems leaders often operate under intense pressure to justify these expenses, while at the same time keeping their costs under control. One of the most straightforward ways to justify these expenses is by demonstrating that information systems are automating work that an organization would otherwise need to employ humans to do.

There are many decisions out there where either the answer is so clear that expert human judgment really isn't necessary or the difference in outcomes is so trivial that it doesn't make sense to spend a lot of human effort on them. But even when the consequences of a set of actions are much more important, human judgment may not be desirable. A good example is infection control in hospitals. There are specific behaviors that make a big difference in the spread of infections. Hand washing immediately comes to mind. In many cases, we do not want people making decisions about whether to wash their hands: we instead want to make it as easy as possible for them to do so, and as hard as possible not to.

Protocolizing is the act of turning a set of decisions into a protocol: a set of defined steps for completing a given task. If decisions can be safely protocolized, they can be made more efficient, because unnecessary decision-making steps can be removed. And if the human decision-making steps can be removed, the remaining steps may be good candidates for *automation*, giving them to a computer or machine to do instead of a human.

Automation has made great strides over the years, especially recently. Some fear that automation is becoming a bit too successful. When the automation benefits us directly, it is easier to be excited about it. Automated tax software is a good example. I take that back—it is a *great* example. Who wouldn't want a technology that takes something awful and tedious off our plates? But when the automation creates hardships for others, that's another story. Many worry about automation destroying jobs. Take self-driving cars and trucks, for instance. Proponents of automation will point to the promise of better safety and the benefit of lower-cost transportation. However, more than 3.5 million people work as truck drivers in the United States alone (Cheeseman and Hait 2019). If an entire category of jobs disappears, what happens to the people who were doing them?

On that note, I have some good news and also some bad news. (Since they are both about the same thing, maybe I should just call them "news.") In the past, whenever a particular job has been automated, it has not necessarily led to mass unemployment— at least not in the long term. In fact, in the long term, automation has generally led to more human work, not less. A good example is the automated teller machine, or ATM for short. When these machines first appeared in the 1970s, there were more than 300,000 bank tellers working in the United States. Many people were convinced that bank tellers were about to lose their jobs. By 2010, some 40 years later, there were more than 400,000 ATMs, and not just in banks. They were showing up in grocery stores and pharmacies as well as many places where people might have been better off without ready access to their cash (casinos, for example). But the tellers didn't disappear—in fact, their numbers had almost doubled. It turned out that ATMs made it cheaper and easier for banks to open new branches, and operate them profitably. As a result, more branches were opened, and more tellers were hired to work in them (Bessen 2015).

So this is good news if you like higher employment, and not-so-good news if you are trying to make the case for an information system investment saving human effort. Returning to healthcare, we can again pick on EHRs. A lot of very important advancements have been made possible by the EHR: greater patient safety; faster, higher-quality clinical research; and easier access to one's own health information. You may notice that this list does not include less work. In fact, since the advent of the EHR, many clinicians (physicians, especially) have found that they need to do even more work, particularly around learning the new systems, participating in changes to them, and documenting the care they are giving to patients. Some physicians have even begun hiring medical clerks to help with some of these steps. (See a familiar pattern here?)

Cybersecurity offers another example of how making things easier can also make them harder. Just like e-commerce made it more feasible for hackers to steal credit card information, EHRs have made it more feasible for hackers to steal patient information. And as it turns out, EHR data are even more valuable to thieves than credit card numbers. Medical records contain so much valuable personal information that they have been called an "identity thief's dream" and have been known to sell on the dark web for hundreds of dollars apiece (CBS Interactive 2019). And that's not the only threat organizational leaders need to worry about. Over the past several years, close to 200 health systems have been affected by *ransomware*, programs installed by hackers that prevent system access until a ransom is paid (Bischoff 2020). In all, more than 80 percent of hospital information security leaders reported having a significant security incident within the past 12 months (HIMSS 2019). As a result, health systems now spend an average of 5 percent of their information systems budgets on safeguarding against these types of threats (Schencker 2019).

Getting the most out of information systems requires substantial planning, careful investment, and ongoing monitoring. As with the employment life cycle, management of information systems can be described as following a system development life cycle (SDLC). Taking the HR analogy a bit further, you might imagine new hardware and software being "hired" (purchased or licensed), "onboarded" (installed and people trained to use them), and "retired" (decommissioned). As with employment, an information systems department will need to manage multiple SDLCs simultaneously, each at different phases of the process. Given the size of the investments we are often talking about, this life cycle also needs to plug into the organization's annual and longer-term budget cycles.

As with the other cycles I described in this chapter, different organizations describe their SDLCs differently, usually identifying somewhere between 4 and 10 steps. The length of time each

4.4 Information system life cycle

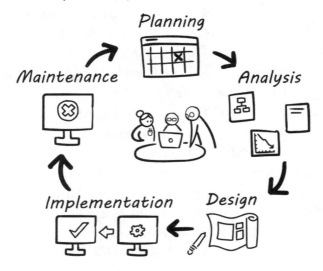

step takes will also vary widely, depending on factors such as the system's complexity, how much training and/or new hiring will be required to run it, and how much end-user input is needed along the way. For our purposes, I will present a general model involving five steps (see figure 4.4).

The first step, *planning*, involves collecting descriptions of the needs people have across the organization that could be addressed through either new systems or upgrades to existing ones. This collection process typically identifies more needs than the organization can afford to address, so the planning stage also involves prioritizing which opportunities seem most important to the organization's overall success. In the second step, *analysis*, the highest-priority needs are examined more closely in order to identify any specific requirements a system solution will need to be able to meet. These needs are then converted into specific plans during step three, *design*. In the fourth step, *implementation*, the new system (or changes to the old one) is rolled out to the organization. Once the system has been fully implemented, it enters the *maintenance* stage, during which its performance is monitored on an ongoing basis as part of the broader monitoring function the information systems department oversees.

If you were to ask your information systems friends what they think of my description of the SDLC, they are likely to say that I am almost criminally simplifying what in reality is a very complicated process indeed. Of all the ways the process is far more complicated than I just described, one of the biggest relates to the system's end users. Successfully bringing a system through these steps requires engaging end users just about every step of the way in what can be a very labor-intensive process. It is also a process that is not always very interesting for the end users to participate in. In fact, some end users will try their best to duck out of providing their input, choosing instead to use that time to focus on tasks that feel more impactful and urgent to them. But doing so only makes information systems people's jobs harder, and the success of the entire SDLC process less certain.

At this point, you should have a good high-level overview of some of the main operating cycles powering all health systems. In the next chapter we will look at the third and final enabling discipline: *self-development.* But first, if you are interested in further strengthening your health system literacy, I want to provide you with some recommendations.

Strengthening Health System Literacy: Learning through Experience

One of the best ways to develop health system literacy over time is to join several industry e-mail lists and commit to reviewing them on a consistent basis. (If you already receive more e-mails than you prefer, you can get the same benefits from committing a specific time weekly to reviewing news updates on a website.) *Becker's Hospital Review* is a free-to-access online news aggregator with a particularly broad reach, and it includes sections devoted specifically to finance, HR, and IT. In terms of original reporting, *Modern Healthcare* is probably the most widely read trade publication among healthcare executives. *Modern Healthcare* also has a free e-mail list service; however, accessing its articles requires a subscription, and it is pricey. Many healthcare executives I know have subscriptions to the weekly print version delivered to their office; you may be able to find someone in your organization who is willing to give you their copies after they finish them.

Mentors and Role Models

You can also gain a deeper understanding of the health system by developing learning relationships with people involved with the major functional areas in your organization. Although good mentors can be found in many different roles, people involved with training and development functions are particularly likely to be interested in sharing what they know. Human resources generally, and employee and organization development departments specifically, can be a good place to start; these individuals may also have suggestions about other knowledgeable, and approachable, people elsewhere in your organization. You can find suggestions about how to engage these individuals productively in appendix 1.

Resources for Learning More

In addition to the news services I mentioned earlier, there are professional associations related to each of the major functional areas of health systems. As with the news services, most will have e-mail lists and association updates you can access from their websites. For human resources, the Society for Human Resource Management (www.shrm.org) is the main professional society; the American Society for Healthcare Human Resource Administration (www.ashhra.org) is more tailored to health systems specifically. For finance, there is the Healthcare Financial Management Association (www.hfma.org). The Health Information Management Systems Society (www.himss.org) is a good one to take a look at for information systems.

If you are interested in an even deeper dive into health system literacy, consider completing one of the massively open online courses (MOOCs) available on this topic. A good example is "Healthcare Delivery Providers" by Dr. Rahul Koranne (2020) from the University of Minnesota, offered on the Coursera platform. If you have the funds to invest in a textbook (or have access to a good library), consider picking up a text from an introduction to healthcare course in an MBA or MHA program. I particularly recommend any recent edition of *The Well-Managed Healthcare Organization*, by Kenneth White and John Griffith. This text is also used by the American College of Healthcare Executives as part of its fellowship program. Finally, if you are interested in a longer-term perspective on how we got to the health system we have today, I recommend *The Social Transformation of American Medicine* by Paul Starr. This Pulitzer Prize–winning book covers the period 1760 to the time of its publication in the early 1980s and to this day is still discussed by health system CEOs. I warn you it is not a quick read, but no other book I am aware of provides quite the same depth of history on this topic.

CHAPTER 5

Self-Development

I n the context of leadership, self-development relates to how
you manage yourself as a resource. Three particularly important competencies support the discipline of self-development:
self-awareness, *self-confidence*, and *well-being*. Since self-awareness is
foundational to the other two, we will start there.

Self-Awareness

Self-awareness involves developing and maintaining an accurate
view of your strengths and development needs, particularly related to how you come across to the people you work with.
Developing self-awareness is not a straightforward process. It
typically involves not only learning new things but also managing any number of *self-deceptions*: self-perceptions that may feel

5.1 The acting vs. judging brain

correct to you, but other people would describe as inaccurate (Sitzmann et al. 2010). Self-deceptions exist because of some fundamental limitations of the hardware of our brains—in particular, much of the activity of our minds is simply inaccessible to our conscious awareness (Wilson and Dunn 2004). While I don't want to turn this into a chapter on neuroscience, the concepts are important enough for some high-level discussion.

Figure 5.1 is a wildly oversimplified map of a human brain. (If you showed this to the professors who raised me, they would probably try to revoke my diploma. Please don't do that.) It is not to scale or accurate in any other way, except to make a point about two things involving different parts of the brain. The component labeled "my actions" is responsible for driving my behavior. The other part, "judgment of others," interprets the actions I see other people taking. You can think of these as separate parts of the brain, which are not wired together in any particularly useful way. In other words, I can't really use the "judgment" module to evaluate my own "actions" module. (If you are interested in experiencing what this disconnect feels like, try self-evaluating your public speaking skills while presenting in front of a mirror.)

Despite this reality, most of us manage to come up with a pretty good story about what we think we are all about. It feels compelling, but often it is not terribly accurate. And the story can get reinforced over time, because we will tend to remember the feedback we get that confirms it, and discard the feedback that does not (Hart et al. 2009). We may even start avoiding people who try to give us disconfirming feedback (Green, Gino, and Staats 2017). To some degree these biases are functional, especially if they help us maintain a healthy level of self-confidence (a topic we will turn to in the next section). But they can also interfere with our ability to learn from our mistakes, which is critical for becoming a more effective leader.

Creating an accurate self-awareness, it turns out, is not really possible through self-reflection directly. It requires help from other people. In effect, we need to "borrow" the perceptions of other people to create more accurate perceptions of ourselves (see figures 5.2 and 5.3).

5.2 One person acts, the other judges

5.3 Self-awareness is developed

In chapter 2, I described the fastest path to better leadership involving both practice and high-quality feedback on that practice. When it comes to interpersonal activities in particular, there are important limitations to our ability to self-assess accurately. Without accurate feedback, our development will be much slower. This is why other people play such an important role in developing self-awareness, particularly when it comes to leadership. The people you work with are in a much better position than you are to reflect on your actions, make judgments about them, and then (assuming you have made them comfortable doing so) give you the perspective that your hardware limitations prevent you from creating for yourself.

All of the above is much easier said than done. Most of us do not really enjoy getting critiqued by others, especially about something so fundamental to our identities as our ability to lead. If I take the feedback too seriously, it can feel devastating—like maybe I am not cut out to lead after all. But if I don't take it seriously enough, then I am not learning what I need from it. This is an area where the next competency, *self-confidence*, is particularly relevant.

Self-Confidence

In the context of leadership, *self-confidence* means believing in your ability to successfully accomplish what you set out to do. The role of self-confidence in leadership success is best understood by reflecting back on our discussion of leadership development in chapter 2. There I described the fastest path to more effective leadership as involving (1) more and better practice, (2) high-quality feedback on that practice, and (3) productive reflection on that feedback in preparation for more practice. All else being equal, someone who is higher in self-confidence is more likely to take the initiative to seek out challenging assignments, and

5.4 Levels of confidence

Underconfident *Confident* *Overconfident*

- *Avoids challenges that may lead to criticism*
- *Feels devastated by critical feedback*

- *Accepts risk and seeks out new challenges*
- *Takes feedback and incorporates it*

- *Takes on challenges without considering risk*
- *Dismisses feedback*

therefore get more practice in these roles. If you have a greater belief that you will succeed at something, you are also likely to persevere longer, which, regardless of outcome, means you are getting more practice. Self-confidence also serves as an emotional buffer for critical feedback: it is less likely to feel devastating, and therefore can be more readily internalized (see figure 5.4).

In the context of leadership, self-confidence plays another important role: maintaining and enhancing the confidence of other people. However, when it comes to leader self-confidence, too much of a good thing is definitely no longer a good thing. *Overconfidence*, consistently overestimating one's capabilities and/ or the likelihood of success, can be an especially thorny problem in leadership roles. Although people are more likely to initially trust a leader who seems more confident, if the leader's judgment proves inaccurate, that trust can disappear quickly (Fleenor et al. 2010).

While it is not always so easy to tell the difference between healthy self-confidence and overconfidence, attitudes toward feedback can provide important clues. A leader with healthy self-confidence will still show an ability to listen openly to the fears and concerns of others. An overconfident leader, on the other hand, will be quicker to dismiss these concerns as baseless and not worth their time to talk about. In more extreme cases, the overconfident leader may react to concerns with open hostility, interpreting them as personal attacks rather than appeals to reason, in a fashion similar to the overinvolved leader I described in chapter 3.

Building Self-Confidence

Self-confidence is so closely related to the learning process that it has been studied extensively by educational scholars and other social scientists. This research suggests that self-confidence gets developed in relation to four specific activities. The first, *mastery experiences*, affects self-confidence most directly and involves successfully completing tasks and activities. Success is the key here: activities do not build your self-confidence if you do not succeed at them. You not only need to succeed but also need to know you were successful, making recognition a critical ingredient as well. The second activity, *social modeling*, involves seeing other people who are similar to you successfully accomplishing an activity. Chances are you have some firsthand experience with this one. Have you ever encouraged a friend of yours to go first when doing something scary for the first time? Crossing a suspiciously old footbridge, or bungee jumping, or the like? If so, and if you felt a sense of relief when your friend survived, you are familiar with what social modeling can do for you. The third activity is *social persuasion*: other people cheerleading us along, giving us a sense that we can do it. This could be a mentor, a trusted colleague, or a good friend. It could also be in the form of a team rallying each other before an important event.

The final activity, *psychological response*, comes from within and involves your ability to summon a positive emotional state in preparation for a challenging task. This is an important part of the "inner game" of leadership: becoming a source of self-confidence not only for yourself but also for the people you work with so that you can also be the source of social modeling and social persuasion. Developing and maintaining these psychological resources relates closely to the final self-development competency: *well-being.*

Well-Being

Well-being is one of those concepts that have about as many working definitions as there are people thinking on the topic. So before going too far, I want to make sure we are working from the same definition. At its most basic level, well-being can be defined as having a sense of contentment in how one is doing, lately and in life generally. Note that this definition relates less to how you are *actually* doing and more to how you *feel about* how you are doing. If you know someone who seems endlessly dissatisfied even though they seem to have it all, or if you know someone who always seems chipper no matter what life throws at them, you have seen this distinction firsthand. Researchers use the term "subjective well-being" to make this point. They also note that contentment has two sides: positive emotions and the absence of negative ones (Deiner 2009). Thus, my use of the word "contentment" in our definition.

Well-being is widely recognized as foundational to good health. In fact, the World Health Organization (n.d.) includes well-being in defining what health is: "a state of complete physical, mental and social well-being and not merely the absence of disease or infirmity." The U.S. Centers for Disease Control and Prevention regularly uses subjective well-being to monitor the success of its public health initiatives. Over time it has found that these measures predict a whole host of other important outcomes, such as mental and physical health, healthy behaviors, productivity, social connectedness, and longevity (U.S. Centers for Disease Control and Prevention, n.d.). I could go on and on here. Frankly, I am tempted to. After all, if our health systems are in the business of health, and well-being is so central to health, doesn't that mean we also need to be in the business of well-being?

As it turns out, our recent history suggests that health systems haven't taken well-being as seriously as they need to. In the years leading up to the COVID-19 pandemic, many health systems had already been grappling with widespread emotional, physical, and mental exhaustion from prolonged stress, also known as burnout. The problem was particularly apparent among physicians who, despite their professional focus on health, had rates of burnout, depression, and suicidal ideation that were significantly higher—and quality of life that was significantly lower—than the population at large (Dyrbye et al. 2014). Physician burnout had also been identified as a risk factor for a wide range of other problems, including increased medical errors, lower patient satisfaction, poorer physician health and self-care, and increased likelihood of quitting the profession altogether (West, Dyrbye, and Shanafelt 2018).

Barriers to well-being do not appear to be unique to physicians, or to health systems in the United States (Woo et al. 2020). To a certain degree, some of these barriers have been woven into the culture of how health systems operate, related to the types of people who get called to serve, and how they are educated and socialized into their roles. Meaningfully improving well-being within health systems is going to require both individual and organizational change. As discussed in chapter 1, the imperative to do so seems likely to become ever stronger in the years ahead.

Managing Well-Being

Taking care of your own well-being is critical to doing your best work and helping others do theirs. A comprehensive discussion of this topic is far beyond the scope of this chapter, but at a high level it involves developing three important habits. The first is regularly taking stock of how you are doing physically, emotionally, and socially. Periodic checkups with a primary care provider will help with the first. Developing good habits around what you eat and drink, appropriate exercise, and consistent quality sleep are also important for maintaining physical health. Developing a better understanding of your sources of joy and fulfillment, as well as aggravation and frustration, will help in maintaining your emotional well-being. Practices such as regular reflection, meditation, progressive muscle relaxation, and gratitude will build psychological resources, allowing you to stay balanced in emotionally challenging times. Social supports are another important source of resilience in the face of hardship. Routinely building positive and productive social interactions into your calendar can be helpful, as well as ensuring your relationships outside the workplace receive the attention they need to flourish.

Cultivating Well-Being in Others: The Leader's Role

Leadership roles are particularly potent social models; as a leader, practicing good personal habits around well-being helps the people you work with do the same. Beyond self-care, leaders who are good at developing a work climate that supports well-being can make a big difference in the lives of everyone they work with. Leaders who formally manage other people are in a position to manage how their employees' work evolves over time. Understanding the elements of jobs that make them more rewarding, frustrating, joyful, or stressful puts leaders in a better position to influence their development in more positive directions. It is especially important to anticipate the impact that organizational changes can have on staff, and to look for signs of unintended consequences. We will return to this topic in chapter 9 on transformation.

Beyond Preserving, toward Growth

The COVID-19 pandemic elevated health system leaders' interest in employee well-being, recognizing the hardships many had endured, and the long-term effects these hardships may have created. Unfortunately, at least at the time of this writing, some are still hoping for a "recovery" or "return to normal." As discussed earlier, health systems were already facing significant barriers to employee well-being before COVID-19 showed up. Fortunately, some health system leaders are recognizing that new approaches are urgently needed. Many of their staff have struggled through challenges that have changed their perspectives permanently; healing on the road ahead will require taking the time to understand and make peace with these experiences. Ideally, these reflective practices will become more widely recognized as helpful to maintaining well-being in the longer term.

It may be possible to set a higher bar still. Rather than framing hardships as something to recover from, they could be viewed as uniquely valuable catalysts for personal growth. Taken even further, this orientation could be part of a broader strategy of proactively designing the workplace to actively promote health rather than just minimize harm.

If the idea of a truly health-affirming workplace sounds overly optimistic to you right now, consider this: as far back as 2013, the technology company Google was actively experimenting with its workplace design and policies to shape employee behavior, with the explicit goal of helping its employees live measurably longer and healthier lives (Bock 2015). Unlike our health systems, Google's (n.d.) mission is not even about health: it is "to organize the world's information and make it universally accessible and

useful." The goal of the initiative supports Google's mission indirectly by giving it a source of competitive advantage in recruiting and retaining talent. Reflect on that for a moment: salary and
benefits only have value to the extent that they help us meet specific needs. A person will consider a job offer more attractive if
they think it will help them better meet those needs. What if instead of a higher salary you were offered a better life directly?
Suddenly a better salary and benefits might not matter as much.

This chapter finishes our tour of leadership's enabling disciplines, the "inner work" of leadership development. In the next
chapter we begin examining the action disciplines, where the
"outer work" takes place. Before we go, I will provide some additional resources and tips for readers interested in continuing
work on self-development.

Strengthening Self-Development: Learning through Experience

At the start of this chapter, I made the case for the foundational
role of self-awareness in self-development. The surest path to
greater self-awareness is candid feedback from people in a good
position to weigh in on how they see and experience you. Your
best chance of getting the feedback you want is to ask for it. Keeping in mind the many barriers to honesty in the workplace, the
people you want feedback from may need your guidance about
what you are truly interested in. Receiving feedback well (e.g.,
"Thank you, that's really helpful to know" rather than "But . . .
but. . . .") also helps pave the way to more candid feedback in the
future, as does circling back to describe how you have been using the feedback in your development.

To develop your self-confidence, consider setting a specific personal goal to periodically pursue activities requiring you to go
beyond the bounds of your prior experience and expertise: your

"comfort zone." I recommend activities for which failing is not associated with any dire consequences, such as people's lives or the fate of the organization being at risk. (If everything you can think of feels risky to you, you may need to first work on challenging your own assumptions about risk: "What, realistically, is the worst that could happen here, and if it did, how bad would the consequences really be?") Be cautious about taking on things that seem truly impossible. It's better to find things that merely seem very difficult.

In terms of well-being, earlier in the chapter I mentioned this is a clear growth need across our health systems, and offered some suggestions for attending to your own maintenance. Once you have your own house in order, so to speak, I encourage you to consider the ways in which your work and workplace support—and detract from—healthy habits. If you can identify a particularly substantial barrier to well-being in the workplace, consider working with your manager and/or others already sympathetic to these concerns to develop strategies for removing these barriers. Finally, if your organization has a leader who is identified as the "chief well-being officer" or something similar, consider finding out how you might help champion the leader's efforts to build a healthier workplace. Often these individuals and their departments have ambitions that are greater than their budgets, so they can use all the like-minded allies they can find.

Mentors and Role Models

A good strategy for spotting great self-development role models is to identify people who seem to maintain an even-temperedness despite having roles that seem highly stressful. Another good source is people who seem to take genuine joy in their work, or at least complain much less about it than everyone around them. Find an opportunity to pick their brain, have them walk you through how they approach their work, and ask them how they keep a level head. You could also ask if they pursue any of the other habits and tactics I have recommended in this chapter, and how these practices help them.

Resources for Learning More

In the area of self-confidence, I can recommend two books that other healthcare leaders have found helpful. For tools and tips on facing hardships with courage, *Dare to Lead* by Brené Brown has been recommended consistently by former students. If you are interested more specifically in strengthening your self-advocacy, consider *Brag! The Art of Your Own Horn without Blowing It* by Peggy Klaus.

If you would like to take a deeper dive into self-awareness, there is a terrific MOOC on the Coursera platform called "Inspiring Leadership through Emotional Intelligence" by Richard Boyatzis from Case Western Reserve University. The course emphasizes practice exercises and also covers mindfulness techniques.

For personal well-being, a very good place to start is with a primary care provider or employee health screen. In addition to whatever resources you discover directly through those channels, there are many readily available tools to help you develop or improve your well-being habits. In particular, numerous apps, many of which are either free or offer free trials, are available that can help you monitor any health-affirming routines you may be working on. For example, if you are interested in meditation, the trial version of the Headspace app provides guided practice and well-designed reminders. Calm is another example of this type of app. These and related apps may require a subscription after a trial period, which you may find worth the money; but if you can develop your own monitoring habits through the use of your own calendar, you may get all you need from the trial version.

At the organization level, if you are interested in practical strategies for addressing clinician burnout specifically, check out the publication *Taking Action against Clinician Burnout* (National Academies of Sciences, Engineering, and Medicine 2019) and the more recent discussion papers from the National Academies of Science, Engineering, and Medicine. All are available from its website for free. If you would like to learn more about the science of well-being, I recommend the Health-Related Quality of Life website maintained by the U.S. Centers for Disease Control and Prevention (n.d.). Here you can find good summaries of the impact of well-being and learn more about how it is monitored at a national level. Finally, if you are excited by the idea of well-being becoming more central to society, I encourage you to read "Well-Being in All Policies," by Dr. Thomas Kottke and colleagues, which is also available from the CDC website (Kottke, Stiefel, and Pronk 2016).

CHAPTER 6

Relations

Although each leadership discipline is important in its own way, if you had to pick only one to be really good at, my recommendation would be relations. This discipline most directly addresses our question from chapter 2: Why would people want to follow you?

The most straightforward answer to this question is that they believe in what you are trying to accomplish. But what makes them believe? There are many possibilities. For example, they may see you acting in ways that are consistent with their values, and believe you are likely to continue doing so in the future. You may also have done something for them in the past for which they are grateful. Perhaps you complimented their work, acknowledged their efforts, shared your appreciation for something important to them, or made their lives easier or better in some other way.

Doing any of these things can create an expectation that more good things will happen if they stick around, and it will build their interest in reciprocating your support. Although I will break these ideas down further in the pages to come, this core idea—helping the people you work with, and doing what you can to make their lives a bit better—is central to effective leadership in healthcare.

As we discussed in chapter 3, different people can have very different needs, interests, and priorities. For this reason, expertise in the relations discipline involves developing a deeper understanding and appreciation of each person's uniqueness—the competency of *interpersonal understanding*.

Interpersonal Understanding

I made the point earlier that people generally follow leaders because they believe those leaders have their best interests in mind. If someone believes your values and priorities are similar to theirs, it becomes a lot easier to trust that you will do things that are consistent with those values. But what about people who may be very different from you? In these cases, it becomes all the more important to understand those differences well enough to know if you are about to cross them in ways they won't appreciate.

Interpersonal understanding is something most of us think we are better at than we actually are. To a degree, making unrealistic assumptions is probably helpful. Imagine a world where every time we ran into someone, we were confronted with just how little we knew about them, and how very different they might be from us. Imagine further that we felt compelled to understand them better before we could trust them enough to work with them. In such a world, we might get to know our coworkers really well, but working with anyone new would require quite a bit of time. When would we get around to the actual work at hand?

Realistically, we have little choice but to make assumptions—a lot of them—about how the people we work with think and feel. The assumption we most often default to is that other people's thoughts and reactions are similar to our own. Researchers refer to this as the *false consensus effect*, and it is remarkably difficult to overcome (Mullen 1983). To make any headway at all against this bias, you first need to recognize it exists. You then need to work actively against the assumption. A good strategy for accomplishing this is to learn more about the general ways people tend to differ, particularly as these differences may play out in workplace interactions.

Personality and Interests

Although personality and individual differences are topics that fill books all by themselves, I can give you a good introduction to one particularly robust model: the RIASEC, originally developed by John Holland (see figure 6.1). The RIASEC model is most frequently used to help people identify jobs and careers that will be a good fit for their interests and styles. Its use has been supported by many decades of research (Hoff et al. 2018). In fact, the U.S. Department of Labor identifies a RIASEC coding for each of the occupations it tracks, and provides an online survey that you can use to identify your own RIASEC code for free (National Center for O*NET Development, n.d.).

The model has six components: realistic, investigative, artistic, social, enterprising, and conventional. RIASEC spells each of them out in relation to the others. Completing a RIASEC assessment gives you a two- or three-letter coding that describes the components of the model that best fit your interests. Adjacent styles on the diagram tend to correlate most closely to one another, so a person's code most often contains adjacent letters. The styles opposite one another on the diagram, in contrast, tend to represent individual differences and usually do not show up in

6.1 The RIASEC personality model

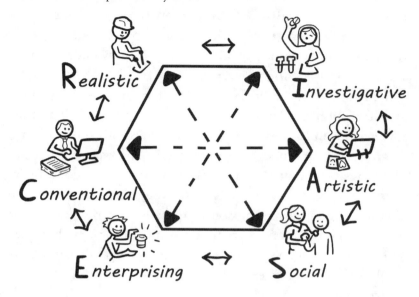

the same profile. This also suggests that individuals with opposing styles are more likely to have complementary rather than overlapping skills. In my descriptions of each of the styles, I illustrate how these opposites can complement one another in health system settings.

Starting with the upper-left corner of the diagram, someone with *realistic* interests tends to enjoy working with "things" (tools, raw materials). Auto repair, plumbing, and carpentry are classic examples of realistic work. In healthcare settings, surgery and laboratory work tend to align with the realistic component of the model. On the opposite side of the diagram is *social*, indicating interests in caring for and nurturing people. Nursing and social work are good examples of occupations that fit well with social interests. Although people can have both realistic and social interests, more typically they gravitate toward one over the other, since they tend to involve very different focal activities. For example, a scientist who people describe as "always in the lab" may simply enjoy realistic activities more than social ones. Since we also tend to get better at the things we practice most, people who are especially good at realistic activities may not be as good at social activities, and vice versa.

Going now to the upper right of the diagram, *investigative* interests share some overlap with realistic ones, in that they both involve a focus on "things." Investigative interests are more oriented toward science and discovery, in the service of a quest for deeper knowledge. Many of the medical disciplines are a good fit for investigative types. Its opposite on the diagram, *enterprising*, has an emphasis on power and social influence. Entrepreneurs and business managers are particularly compatible with the enterprising style. Over the years, I have seen many good examples of people with investigative and enterprising styles working together to accomplish things neither could do alone. In academic medical centers, technology commercialization offices immediately come to mind. A researcher with an investigative style may mainly care about being able to do her research; activities such as managing the lab and paying the bills may be experienced mainly as distractions from her interests. Left to her own devices, she might never get around to letting the business world know about her discoveries, and instead stick to running experiments (at least until the funding runs out). Conversely, a commercialization specialist with an enterprising style might look at every lab experiment through the lens of questions like: Who could make money off this discovery? How might we most quickly "monetize" it for our organization? What is the best way to showcase its commercial potential? With his help, our researcher may be in a better place to find ongoing support for her work. However, without investigative types to balance him out, the institution might only pursue research with clear revenue potential, and the academic mission of the institution would be diminished.

Our last pair of opposites are *artistic* and *conventional*. Conventional interests relate to putting things in order, including developing and following protocols. Classic examples of conventional careers in health systems include accountants, compliance officers, and health information techs. Artistic interests, in contrast, gravitate toward the opposite: taking new approaches to things, also known as "coloring outside the lines." Of the six interest types, artistic is the least frequently seen in the healthcare professions. However, the value of artistic interests and professions within healthcare is widely recognized, and, in recent years, more artistically oriented disciplines such as human-centered design have been finding their way into healthcare. As our health systems continue to become more consumer centered, I anticipate this trend will continue, and may even accelerate.

Although the RIASEC and other models of personality and interests offer a good starting point for understanding people, they are only a window into a vast diversity of individual differences. Getting a better understanding of the specific people you work with also requires developing a greater sensitivity to what they may already be expressing. Honing skills in active listening can be particularly helpful to gaining this better understanding.

Active Listening

Active listening, or "listening like you mean it" (Dye and Garman 2015), involves approaching people with a sense of appreciation and curiosity, and a genuine interest in knowing them better because they deserve your attention. A key ingredient of active listening involves training yourself to focus intently on what other people are saying, and sustaining that focus as best you can throughout the course of your conversations. Doing this well requires real effort and a lot of practice. Our human hardware is against us on this: we are able to process speech at a rate much faster than people are able to speak, so our brains often end up looking for other things to do while waiting for the next batch of words. A less disciplined mind will quickly wander off to other topics, like planning for the next meeting or what to eat after work, for example. If we let our minds wander too much, they may find things to think about that are a lot more interesting than the conversation at hand, making it all the more difficult to come back in time to catch and comprehend the next few words.

Several techniques can help us stay focused while we are actively listening. Hands down the best one to start with, if you haven't already done so, is making sure your phone (or other mobile device) is not in a place where it might accidentally find its way back to your eyeballs.

Seriously now, if you are already in the habit of putting your phone away when you are engaging with other people, congratulations (and please feel free to skip over the next paragraph). If you are among the many people who have not developed this habit, please continue reading. It's for your own good, and I'll try to keep it short.

Mobile devices are an excellent example of a "progress trap" (Wright 2005), a technology whose continued evolution starts to work against us, and we have not yet figured out how to manage that reality. Although they offer tremendous benefits, they are continually evolving to command as much of our attention as possible, and over a very short time they have found remarkable success. A national survey from 2017 found that the average American checks their phone 80 times a day; just two years later, the frequency was up 20 percent to 96 times a day (Asurion 2019). Although it is tempting to believe we can divide our attention between multiple tasks at the same time, research on brain functioning suggests otherwise. A growing body of evidence shows people who spend more time "multitasking" with their phones end up with everything from lower GPAs (Alghamadi et al. 2020) to more frequent bicycle and car accidents (Stavrinos et al. 2018). There is even evidence that our phones drain our attention just by being in a place we can see them, even if we are not checking them (Ward et al. 2017)! Beyond distraction, increased smartphone use has also been linked to greater anxiety and depression, as well as lower quality of sleep (Jiaxin et al. 2020). Perhaps most importantly in leadership, a growing body of research has found that people tend to react strongly and negatively when they see someone they are interacting with get distracted by their phone (Courtright and Caplan 2020). Keep in mind, the converse of each of these findings is also true: the undivided attention you create by periodically putting your mobile device away can yield higher grades, lower anxiety and depression, safer travels, and better engagement.

With mobile device habits taken care of, I will discuss the additional active listening techniques in order of relative difficulty. The first and most straightforward is *suspending judgment*. Self-awareness can help a lot with this one. When you notice yourself disagreeing in your head with someone, challenge yourself to take an approach of curiosity in place of argument. Instead of thinking, "Where is this person's thinking flawed?" practice thinking, "I wonder what is causing our perspectives to be so different." It can be helpful to imagine that the two of you occupy somewhat different realities: both are equally valid, and each seems more compellingly real to the person occupying it. If we were to observe someone suspending judgment, what we might see is the person nodding their head and perhaps looking a bit concerned.

Suspending judgment lays the groundwork for the next technique: *inviting further contributions*. People tend to become more or less at ease according to how the people they are speaking to are reacting to them. If you are demonstrating attentiveness (facing the person, making eye contact, nodding your head periodically), the person who is talking to you is much more likely to open up further. Conversely, to the extent that you display either dismay or divided attention (frowning, interrupting to "correct" the person, checking your watch or phone), the person may start to close down.

There is an important verbal component to effectively inviting further contributions. It involves asking—and, in certain circumstances, interrupting with—questions designed to help the person zero in on the areas of greatest importance or concern. The phrases you can use for this are pretty straightforward: "Say more about ____," or "Can you expand a bit on ____." What requires practice is sensing when these types of questions may be particularly helpful in steering the conversation, and where the focal points may be.

Although these types of questions can be helpful in getting someone talking, sometimes people get stuck on a particular point and have trouble moving forward. In these cases, *paraphrasing content* may be helpful. The idea here is to summarize what the person is saying using your own words, and checking your understanding with them. This technique can be particularly powerful for several reasons. I'll start with the more obvious one: if you repeat back what someone said in your own words, it's about as clear a signal as you can possibly give that you truly heard—and care about—what they had to say (Seehausen et al. 2012). Repeating back their words only confirms hearing, not listening. But taking what they said and putting it in your own words? That's real listening in action. There is another less obvious, and equally powerful, benefit to using this technique. In situations where you disagree with someone, paraphrasing their perspective not only helps convey that you are listening but also helps you better *understand* their perspective and become less deeply rooted in believing your own point of view is the only "correct" one.

The next two techniques involve inference, hazarding a guess as to what is on a person's mind. Guessing is risky business: if you get it wrong, you can come across as less understanding. Framing these techniques using questions can help. The first involves *reflecting the implications*. The inference you are making, and testing out, is whether you understand what the person thinks is the case (or what they think will happen) related to what they are telling you. The phrases are relatively straightforward. For example, "Are you thinking this might mean . . . ," "Are you hoping this might lead to . . . ," "Are you concerned this is going to . . ." The part that requires more practice is identifying the times when using this technique will be most helpful. A good rule of thumb is to wait until after you have summarized content at least once and have received at least some verification that you are on the right track in your understanding.

The last (and trickiest) technique involves *reflecting underlying emotions*—in other words, checking your understanding of how someone is feeling about what they are telling you. Using this technique effectively takes a fair amount of practice, and even experienced active listeners don't get it right all the time. Even when a listener is on the right track, a speaker may sometimes not truly know how they are feeling about something, or, if they do, they may feel very uncomfortable having their feelings pointed out to them, especially if they view emotions as a source of vulnerability. You can make these "guesses" less threatening if you frame them in terms of how either you or other people would generally feel under the same circumstances. For example, "If that happened to me, I think I would be pretty upset about it," or "I imagine that would be pretty aggravating."

The benefits of active listening extend beyond honing your own interpersonal understanding. The people who are listened to benefit as well. Feeling listened to in the workplace has been linked to numerous well-being and performance benefits, including a heightened sense of psychological safety and increased creativity (Castro et al. 2018). In terms of leadership, better listeners are also demonstrably more successful at the next competency: influencing others (Ames, Maissen, and Brockner 2012).

Power and Influencing

When I use the terms "power" and "influence," what do you think of? If you imagined a group of shadowy figures in a back room making deals over who controls the world, you are not alone (Hall 2016). Power and influence are very important concepts related to leadership, but they tend to get a bad reputation. Like loaded dice, they are sometimes seen as tools people use to "cheat" in order to get what they want. In truth, power and influence are realities of leadership roles, and they are neither inherently good nor inherently bad. The good and bad mainly relate to how they are used. To better understand how to use them as tools for good, we first need to agree on a set of definitions. This is not an easy step, especially since both "power" and "influence" can be used as both nouns and verbs.

For our purposes, I will define *power* in a leadership context the same way you might think about power in a nine-volt battery: as a measure of stored energy, something that can be used later for a variety of purposes. In this sense, you could imagine a high-powered person as someone with an unusually large and fully charged battery. In contrast, I will define *influence* (or *influencing*, if that makes the distinction clearer) as the *use* of that power to make something happen. The battery provides the *power*; the tool the battery gets inserted into does the *influencing*.

As with batteries, power in leadership is not a permanent state. It needs to be recharged periodically or it will be depleted. This recharging can come from different sources, which are also important to understand. Six sources of power are particularly relevant to leadership in organizations (French and Raven 1959). The most familiar of these is *legitimized power*; you can think of it as "power by job description." The job you hold with an organization grants you certain rights and expectations, which are an important form of power. Although people tend to think of this as the main source of power in organizations, it is really only useful within a limited scope of applications. On the one hand, managers are allowed to order their direct reports to do certain job-related things. On the other, people generally don't like being ordered around, and will tolerate only so much of that. So the legitimized power battery tends to get depleted quickly and is slow to recharge. In the meantime, the other sources of power need to be used.

Another familiar power source is *reward power*, the ability to provide benefits or rewards: "If you do this for me, I will give you ____." Along with reward power is its evil twin *coercive power*, the ability to bring on consequences: "Do this for me or else I'll ____." At this point, you may be starting to see how power sources can work together in important ways. If you have legitimized power as a manager, the role probably comes with some access to coercive power and reward power. However, people can also have reward and/or coercive power without having legitimate power. Reward power only requires access to things that other people want. Coercive power only requires the ability to control the flow of things happening that a person doesn't want. For example, if publicity is important to a given employee, a company's newsletter editor may have both reward and coercive power over the employee, without any legitimized power. In a healthcare setting, reward power could be associated with a clinician or team's ability to generate revenue for the organization, or a process improvement team's ability to make people's work easier.

To some degree, every single person working in an organization has some amount of reward power in their role, regardless of their formal title. The power comes in the form of our *discretionary effort*, the amount of effort we decide to put into our work beyond the minimum necessary. (If you want to see just how powerful reward power can be in action, look for some ways you might make your boss's job easier for them, and then offer to do them.)

Legitimized, reward, and coercive power can be rather blunt instruments. The next three power sources are more subtle. *Expert power* comes from a person's specialized knowledge or expertise. In healthcare organizations in particular, expert power can be very potent indeed. If you work in such a setting, you may have noticed a few people who are particularly noteworthy in their discipline holding greater sway than would be expected based on their formal title. Expert power is sometimes confused with the similar-sounding *information power*, but the two are distinct. Unlike expert power, which is generally a property of the individual, information power focuses more on access to a resource. A person can have information power from, for example, participating on an important decision-making committee in the organization, or from knowing people who are working on an initiative that will have broad impact on others. If people seek you out for updates on what's going on, you have some information power based on what you know.

The final source, *referent power*, is the most difficult to clearly define. It relates mainly to general likability, respect, and/or admiration. A person with referent power is someone no one wants to disappoint—not because of the personal repercussions but because it just wouldn't feel right. Political offices tend to be held by people with a lot of referent power; politicians need to be liked in order to be elected and reelected. Referent power can grow along with organizational tenure, especially for people who take the time to develop good working relationships across the organization.

Positive Influencing: Helping People Develop

In the chapter on self-development, I pointed out the critical role of self-awareness and why we need other people to help us develop it. The other side of that coin is that *your* perceptions, in a leadership role, will be essential to developing the people you work with. Becoming good at feedback takes a lot of practice. Fortunately, there are some good models as well as science to guide us. Before jumping into it, an important point about feedback style is in order.

Although feedback has been studied extensively by social sciences for many decades, this research took an important turn in 1996. That year, a meta-analysis pulling together more than 600 studies on feedback turned up something unexpected. On the one hand, the study reconfirmed that feedback is critical for improved performance. But the researchers also found that feedback did not always improve performance; in fact, almost one-third of the time it actually *decreased* performance (Kluwer and DeNisi 1996). It turns out that for feedback to be effective, it needs to stick pretty closely to the task at hand—in particular, what is working and what needs to change. Not all feedback does that. Some feedback aims less at what was observed and more at the *why* behind the task: what motivated the person or why they were involved in the task in the first place. The more global that feedback gets, the bigger the risk that it will undermine the receiver's self-confidence. And self-confidence, as we learned in the self-development chapter, is crucial for learning; challenges to self-confidence interfere with the learning process.

Even when feedback is task focused, there is always some risk of hard feelings. But there is even greater risk in routinely avoiding feedback. If problems are not brought to a person's attention, there is no opportunity to fix them; meanwhile, the habits supporting the problem behaviors will continue to strengthen. In the interpersonal context especially, interactions that strain working relationships almost never just go away on their own (if they did, I would have titled this section of the book "How to patiently wait things out"). Usually the best path forward is to err on the side of providing feedback, but with careful attention to design and approach.

Below I provide a set of framing steps for designing feedback to maximize the likelihood that it is fully heard and has its intended impact. The steps aren't a magic spell; you can still deliver effective feedback if you miss a step or two. Following all of the steps doesn't guarantee success—that is always in part up to the person receiving the feedback. If you can, I recommend working through these steps in advance, to give yourself the chance for some revising as needed. If the conversation feels especially risky, it may help to run your approach by a trusted friend or colleague before you go live with the conversation.

A specific example will help illustrate the steps. In this example, you are a relatively new manager, and Pat, one of your direct reports (or a student intern, if you like), is joining you at a departmental meeting. Lynn, your boss's boss, is there as well. As Lynn begins providing a high-level update about what's going on in your organization, you notice her glancing disapprovingly at Pat. You look over at Pat and notice that he is looking at his phone under the table, carrying on a text conversation. (He seems confident that because his phone is under the table, no one has any idea what he is doing.) You want to give Pat some feedback about what you observed, but you also know Pat can be pretty thin-skinned. We'll now develop an approach for this feedback using seven general steps.

Step 1: Create a Safe Climate

In this context, creating a safe climate means one relatively free from threat. If you are going to talk about something difficult, the last thing you want is for someone to already be on guard before you even begin. For starters, it is best to find a private place to have the conversation, an area that is out of sight and earshot of any audience that might add to the discomfort. From there, give some thought to any potential meaning of places you are considering meeting. For example, telling a direct report to meet you in your office is more likely to heighten concern than if you meet the person in the cafeteria or at an outdoor bench on a sunny day. If you want to be particularly conciliatory, you can ask the person to pick the place and time. For our example with Pat, creating a little discomfort may be useful, and a meeting in your office may be the right choice.

Depending on the nature of the conversation, it may also be helpful to begin the dialogue with something that sets a comfortable tone. In the case of Pat, this could involve a general check-in to see how things are going for him. Alternatively, you could start by discussing a shared aspect of your work together, something that underscores you both being on the same team.

Step 2: State Your Topic of Concern ("I Want to Talk to You About . . .")

What's most important in this step is to identify a shared *context* for your feedback. You will have the chance to provide the actual feedback later on, but first you want to have a shared understanding of purpose for the discussion. In Pat's case, the communication might be something like the following: "I want to talk to you about participation expectations in our departmental meetings." This may sound fine for a direct report, but what if Pat were a peer? In this case, you may want to set a more collegial tone—for example, about helping your peer versus setting expectations. For example: "I'd like to talk to you about something I observed in our last meeting. Knowing how important professionalism is to you, I think you may have come across in a way that you didn't intend."

Step 3: Describe (Behaviorally) What Your Expectation Was, and Why

Getting agreement on shared expectations provides a solid foundation on which to provide your feedback. It also sends the message (a positive one) that you believe the person wants to meet them. It allows you to frame the feedback in the context of benefit—something that can help the person meet the expectations you share. (Without these guardrails, you are much more likely to get one of two defensive reactions: "No, I didn't do that" or "Yeah, I did that. What's the big deal?") Continuing on with the example of Pat, you could choose to make one or more of the following points:

- "The goal of these meetings is for us all to develop a shared understanding of what is happening in the organization so that we can move forward more quickly and efficiently. So when we are all together, everyone's full attention is critically important. Does that seem reasonable?"
- "Organizational leaders don't get to see our day-to-day work. When they visit our department for a meeting, giving them our full attention is particularly important in conveying our support. Does that make sense?"

Ideally, this step ends with the other person agreeing that your expectations are reasonable. In Pat's case, maybe he still doesn't know what he has done that led to this conversation, but as long as he is agreeing on the principles, the groundwork you are laying should help you get there very soon.

Step 4: Describe What You Observed

In this step, you want to articulate what you saw, as objectively as possible. In the example of Pat, you noticed Lynn's reaction, and then Pat's texting. These are much better talking points than, say, "I saw you being very rude," which is an *interpretation* of what you saw, and a more global judgment. Stick as best you can to what you saw, and leave the interpretations out of it.

If step 4 goes well, you may have helped the person correct a blind spot in their perception, and you will now have agreement on the facts. If it does not go well, you may have observed something that was too far outside the person's own experience for them to recognize, or perhaps even believe. At worst, the person may try to completely deny the validity of your observations. In Pat's case, he may try to argue that he was just responding to a single text, even though you are certain you saw him going back and forth on his phone for several minutes. If that happens, it is generally inadvisable to try to prove you are correct. A gentler path is to note that your observations are just that, your observations, and then underscore your main points about the importance of meeting behavior. "Look, maybe you weren't on your phone as long as it seemed to me in the moment—I do tend to be on heightened alert whenever my boss's boss is in the room. It's an important survival skill. The point I want to make is about being fully attentive in these types of meetings. Let's just stick with that."

Step 5: Seek a Shared Understanding

If you have worked through each of the prior steps, chances are you have completed most of the heavy lifting already, and the rest of the conversation can be more collegial. In the prior steps you agreed on the topic at hand, its importance, and the gap between expectations and what you observed; you can now shift to some collaborative problem solving about how to best close that gap. Sometimes the original problem stems from a simple lack of shared understanding of expectations, and clarifying expectations is itself enough. Other times additional barriers may need to be addressed, such as developing additional skills or getting access to information or other resources. Examples of good framing questions for this step include "Is this something you are confident you can address going forward?" "How might I best help you address the barriers you described?"

In our example of Pat, pointing out the concern may be all he needs to modify his own actions. But he might identify some specific barriers he's concerned about—for example, thinking he needs to monitor some work-related activity happening outside the meeting (you might need to give him explicit permission to set aside the responsibility during the meeting), having trouble managing his own attention (you might suggest some focusing exercises he can practice), or simply recognizing he has trouble resisting the temptation of checking his phone (you might suggest he turn his phone off during these meetings or at least keep it out of reach).

Step 6: Agree on a Clear Path Forward

After you have talked through any roadblocks and how to address them, it's important to agree on a specific definition of what future success looks like, and the approach to getting there. As with other forms of goal setting, you want to be specific but also realistic. In the example with Pat, agreeing to "never have my phone out at another departmental meeting ever again" is nice and specific but may not be realistic. Setting an "emergencies only" expectation may be a better intermediate step, with an accompanying agreement that if you see him on the phone, you will be asking later what the emergency was.

Step 7: Close in a Supportive Way

In keeping with our prior points about self-confidence, it is helpful to end with a comment or two of support or encouragement. If the conversation went well, this may feel less important, but in general it is more helpful than harmful. In Pat's case, examples of supportive comments could include the following: "I am glad we had this conversation, and appreciate your openness to my feedback." "You have been very good about addressing these kinds of things in the past. I have full confidence in you about this one as well, and I'm here to support you."

Now that you have some new strategies for interpersonal understanding, active listening, and feedback in your toolkit, we will take all these concepts up to the next level: leading teams.

Tying It All Together: Team Leadership

Take a moment to think about teams you have participated on, either in an education setting or in a work setting. If your experiences are like most people's, some teams worked together much better than others. Success in *team leadership* requires bringing the many components of effective leadership together within the context of team interactions. Although "team" can be used to describe any group of people collaborating on shared goals, for our purposes I will focus on a specific type: the temporary team, assembled for a time-limited purpose, whose members are led by someone who is not their formal boss (in other words, someone with little to no legitimized power).

Most teams go through a definable set of developmental stages. While there are numerous models of team life cycles out there,

6.2 Stages of team development

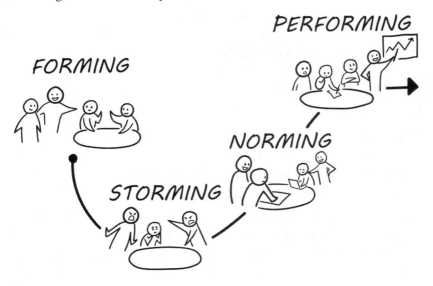

the most widely cited model was developed in the 1960s by Bruce Tuckman (1965) (see figure 6.2). The first stage, *forming*, describes the period when a group first assembles around what they believe are shared goals. This stage can feel very exciting, full of visions of all the possibilities people can accomplish together, as well as all the free time they imagine having to work on these activities in the weeks to come. It is a time when people tend to make assumptions (lots of them) about everyone having more of a shared understanding about things than is actually the case. (Everything we discussed about assumptions in the "Interpersonal Understanding" section also applies in teams; only now, with more people, the effects are multiplied.)

After a feel-good meeting or two, differences in people's unspoken assumptions start to emerge, launching the team into stage two: *storming*. During this stage, team members may feel like the team is "stuck." If anyone on the team is relatively new to these dynamics, this stage can feel downright worrisome to them. But it is a natural part of the team life cycle. It can't be skipped over; it must be worked through. This work may involve taking more time to listen to team members' concerns, making their assumptions more explicit, and negotiating agreements about how best to proceed. The time this process takes can vary considerably. Sometimes a new path can be hammered out in a single meeting. Other times it can take many, many meetings. In some cases, a team never moves past the storming phase. Instead, members realize that their individual interests are collectively incompatible, and perhaps the team never should have been formed in the first place. Sometimes that is the right call.

If a team does prevail through the storming phase, it will be because of members' successful work in the *norming* phase. Norms are the rules, guidelines, and/or shared expectations that the group develops and, eventually, gets comfortable with. Once a group has norms in place, it moves to the *performing* phase, which, as you may have guessed, is when the group actually makes most of its progress on whatever brought it together in the first place.

So there you have it: forming, storming, norming, and performing. (If you like closure, you can add *adjourning* to the end.) As a team leader, it can be helpful to mentally keep track of the stage you think your team is in. Discussing the life cycle with your team can also help them understand why some steps may seem to take longer than they should, but are a normal part of the process. (I'm looking at you, storming.)

Now for some good news: there is a shortcut through the storming stage. It was identified by William Dyer and his colleagues (Dyer, Dyer, and Dyer 2013). It requires you to spend a bit more time in the forming stage, but if you can tolerate that, you can skip a lot of the storming drama and head straight on over to norming and performing. The shortcut is especially useful in teams where you may not already know all of the participants, or where you suspect some may not be very committed. This is a pretty good description of many class projects, as well as work teams involving people who were "volun-*told*" to participate. Here's how it works.

Step 1: Measure Individual Commitment Levels

Before even getting things started, ask each team member to weigh in on (1) how much of a priority their participation is going to be for them, and (2) how much of a time commitment they are willing and able to realistically make to the work. Ask for both in a quantifiable way if you can—for example, priority could be on a scale of 1 (highest priority) to 10 (lowest priority), and time commitment could be hours per week or month. Try to get as honest an answer as you can to both questions; you want realistic responses, not what they think their commitment *should* be. Although this step can be done in a group setting (Dyer recommends this), I have found I get the most honest answers through one-on-one conversations before the first meeting.

Step 2: Discuss Individual Expectations

Once you have these data together, the next step is for the team to discuss individual expectations. This step is best completed as an agenda item for the group during its first meeting. Each member should weigh in on the following: (1) greatest hopes for your work together (what will things look like if we are wildly successful?), (2) greatest fears or concerns (if things don't go as planned, what is most likely to have interfered with success?), and (3) plans for success (what are the most important steps the team can take to head off these potential threats?). Each person on the team should have the opportunity to share their views, and ideally these views should be summarized during the meeting itself for future review. The approach that has worked best for me is "round robin": addressing one question at a time, and going around the table (or video screen) to make sure everyone has responded.

Step 3: Articulate Team Goals

After you have completed the check-in about individual expectations, the next step is to articulate team goals. Said differently: What is the team's mission, and how will you know when it has been accomplished? The mission and goals should be developed into a formal written statement that everyone has the chance to weigh in on, and ultimately agree on. The end goal should be a description of a specific accomplishment that clearly indicates when the work of the team has been completed. Once this end goal has been identified, you can next work with the team to identify a set of specific steps that will be needed to reach this goal.

Step 4: Develop Team Operating Guidelines

After your mission and goals have been agreed on, the fourth and final step is to develop team operating guidelines. These guidelines should, at a minimum, describe how you will approach each of the following four areas: the work itself, decision-making, resolving disagreements, and ensuring everyone is heard. For example, in terms of the work itself, the team might agree that meetings are to be scheduled as working sessions, carving out time to make progress and the opportunity for questions to be clarified. Alternatively, the team might agree that most work should take place over e-mail, with in-person meetings scheduled only when problems come up.

In terms of decision-making, team members should have a sense of when they can make judgment calls independently, and when they should check back with the team and/or team lead. In many cases, it works best to set the expectation that decisions only come back to the team for discussion if they affect either resource needs or other people on the team (e.g., how much time something will take, or the deadlines of other steps). In terms of disagreements, a good approach is to set the expectation that if two or more people on the team have unresolvable differences in opinion about how to proceed, they will call a meeting with the team leader or the entire team to talk through it. Decisions and disagreements could be resolved through consensus discussion, democratic vote, or by the team leader, with different approaches taken based on the nature of what's at stake.

In terms of ensuring everyone is heard, one approach is to simply set the expectation that everyone contributes their perspectives during meetings and when issues come up. At the other extreme, the team might agree for the team leader, or a meeting facilitator, to structure meetings such that a "round robin" check-in with team members is conducted at specific times, and that anyone who is absent is also contacted to collect their input.

Strengthening Relations: Learning through Experience

One of the best ways to strengthen relations skills is by getting involved with leadership roles of all kinds: formal and informal, professional and volunteer. Within organizations, volunteer roles leading process or quality improvement initiatives, community service projects, or employee resource groups can provide exposure to a broader diversity of collaborators and experience tailoring your approaches to people with different priorities and styles of work. If you are interested in building your talent development skills outside of a formal management role, consider working with student interns or serving in a mentoring role. Even if you are relatively early in your career, you can develop these skills through roles in "reverse mentoring," bringing newer skills, experiences, and perspectives to people further along in their careers who need them.

Mentors and Role Models

You can find good role models in leaders who have earned a reputation for developing their staff, especially leaders who are in roles involving lots of direct reports and/or lots of different departments. Chief operating officers and chief nursing officers are good examples of these roles, as are many of the people reporting directly to them. Additionally, people in positions where success hinges on developing influence across many departments also tend to build excellent relationship skills. These can include marketing, internal communications, and organization development, as well as philanthropy.

Resources for Learning More

If you are willing to make a small investment, there are several excellent, inexpensive paperbacks on the topics discussed in this chapter. The team leadership concepts I introduced were heavily influenced by W. Gibb, Jeffrey, and William Dyer's *Team Building: Proven Strategies for Improving Team Performance*. Their book provides highly practical advice on building specific types of teams, as well as solving a variety of problems teams commonly face. In terms of providing feedback, I highly recommend Kerry Patterson and colleagues' book *Crucial Conversations: Tools for Talking When the Stakes Are High*. It is an inexpensive investment for the learning value it contains, which includes numerous walkthrough dialogues on tough topics that illustrate their points. In terms of influence, I highly recommend *Getting to Yes: Negotiating Agreement without Giving In*, by Roger Fisher, William Ury, and Bruce Patton. It is a quick read with many practical tips for finding common ground on the path to agreement. Like Patterson's book, it is available in many public libraries, and I have often spotted copies in the business section of used bookstores.

CHAPTER 7

Execution

In the last chapter, I described the core concepts of the relations discipline as helping the people you work with and doing what you can to make their lives a bit better. For the *execution* discipline, the core concept involves clarifying and carrying out a course of action. Although relations and execution work hand in hand, they are distinct disciplines, and not every leader is good at both. Some leaders are very effective interpersonally but still struggle with the nuts and bolts of getting things done. Other leaders may be remarkable at getting things done, in the short term at least, but may struggle to build the quality of working relationships necessary for long-term success. The most effective leaders strike a good balance between these two disciplines, both in terms of skill and in terms of focus. In this chapter, I will introduce you to some skills and approaches to execution that can make you a more effective leader, especially when combined with effective relations.

Performance Measurement

> If we have data, let's look at data. If all we have are opinions, let's go with mine.
> —*Jim Barksdale*

In order for people to be able to work together toward a common goal, they first need a clear consensus on what that goal is. *Performance measurement* involves identifying appropriate criteria by which progress toward goals can be judged. If a goal can't be measured in a way that people agree on, it will be very difficult indeed to ever agree that the goal has been reached. Thankfully, almost anything can be measured—maybe not as precisely as we'd like, but well enough to form a basis for agreement.

Consider for a moment how you are currently evaluated, at work or at school. If you are a clinician, you may have productivity goals (for example, a specific number of patient visits you are expected to complete on a weekly or monthly basis). You may also have quality goals, such as getting patients in for appointments within a certain amount of time, adhering to practice standards, and writing complete case notes. If you are a student in a class, you may have your goals spelled out in a syllabus: specific assignments with associated point values and, hopefully, some clear guidance about the assignment qualities associated with earning points. If your experiences are like most people's, some of these goals will be clearer and more sensible than others. You will also find some of them more motivating than others. In every case, at some point in the past, someone made the decision that this was the best way to measure performance at the time.

What makes a performance measurement ideal? The simplest answer is that it is the most meaningful and practical method you can find to show progress toward a given mission or vision. Getting to an ideal measurement approach is almost never a one-step process. Typically, once a measure is agreed on and used for a while, its limitations reveal themselves, and a new approach to measurement is required. The following questions can be helpful for identifying these limitations.

1. *What are the biggest differences between the measures we have chosen and our ultimate vision?* Within organizations, departments supporting employees often have gaps between their aspirational goals and how those goals are measured. Employee wellness programs are a good example. Although the vision for a wellness program may be healthier employees, often what is actually measured is the number of programs offered and/or the size of the audiences they draw. On the surface this may seem sensible enough, but in practice, these measures are far removed from actual employee health. We are taking on faith that participation will yield the actual outcomes of interest, but this is usually not the case (Jones, Molitor, and Reif 2019). Of course, an organization needs to start somewhere, but if the end goal is healthier employees, understanding the limitations of current measures is a very important first step toward better ones.

2. *In what ways might the approach to measuring be biased?* This question implies several important related questions. First: Who is doing the measuring? And second: What are the incentives for accuracy (or inaccuracy)? If the person doing the measuring stands to gain from misrepresenting the measure, there is probably some risk they will do so. This phenomenon is sometimes called "gaming the metrics." Customer service metrics are a good example. In one organization I worked with, if I had a computer problem, I would call the help desk and leave a message. The tech

receiving the message was then supposed to open a "ticket" in the tracking system showing the time of the request, which would also alert the customer that the request had been received. Once the problem was resolved, the ticket would be closed, and a receipt of the closure would be sent to the customer. In terms of metrics, one way the information services department evaluated its support technicians was on how quickly they resolved customer issues, which were measured according to the average length of time that tickets were open. However, the techs were also responsible for opening and closing the tickets. This led to all sorts of gaming. Sometimes a tech would wait to open a ticket until after they had reached out to the customer and started working on the problem. I would sometimes see a ticket opened and then closed within the same minute. Their response times looked terrific, but they did not reflect improvements in service, just better gaming.

3. *How might our judgment of progress become biased?* Even in cases where measures are sound and approaches to measurement are objective, we can have biases in the conclusions we draw about our progress. These biases can come from limitations to our measurement approach and also from our emotions. On the measurement side, even with approaches that seem very straightforward on the surface—measuring improvement over time, for example—there is often more to the story than meets the eye. Patient satisfaction measures provide a good example. Most health systems routinely ask patients to complete surveys about experiences with their care. Many health systems use the results to systematically identify care units where satisfaction is lowest and will then focus greater attention on bringing their scores up. On the surface this seems sensible enough: you want to prioritize the biggest problem areas first. What may be counterintuitive is that these same care units are also statistically the most likely to improve on their own, regardless of outside intervention. This is

because of a statistical phenomenon known as *regression toward the mean*: the tendency, over time, for unusually high or low measurements in a normal distribution to move closer to the midpoint of the range (Kane, Maciejewski, and Finch 1997).

On the emotional side, researchers have identified a variety of cognitive biases we deploy to protect our self-esteem, including how we interpret signals of success and failure. For example, when people achieve a goal, they are likely to attribute their success to personal effort; but when they do not achieve a goal, they are likely to conclude that external factors outside their control affected their performance. The bigger the potential threat to one's self-esteem, the stronger this self-serving bias becomes (Campbell and Sedikides 1999).

4. *What important things are our measures not picking up?* Measurement inevitably involves trade-offs between quality, comprehensiveness, and efficiency. We can't measure everything we want to, and anytime we decide to prioritize one set of measures, we are choosing to give less attention to other potentially useful information. Returning to our patient experience example, all patients—as humans—are in some ways unique, and in other ways share a set of common characteristics. Collecting feedback from patients generally involves a trade-off between recognizing each patient as an individual and looking for patterns across them in groups. There is also an upper limit to the time we can reasonably expect patients to spend completing surveys, so we need to identify the limited set of questions that we think will provide the most useful feedback.

From Measuring to Improving: Setting Good Goals

Now that we have discussed the benefits as well as the limitations of measurement, we can consider how to best set goals against these measures. What makes some goals more impactful than others? Researchers have identified several important ingredients (Epton, Currie, and Armitage 2017; Kleingeld, van Mierlo, and Arends 2011). The first is *specificity*. If people are given a specific goal to strive for, their performance is significantly better than if they are simply told to do their best. Psychologically, having a specific target in mind seems to help people focus and can also be motivating as they see progress toward it. Conversely, doing one's best offers no such sense of progress or accomplishment. Did I really do the best I could? How would I ever be sure? The second ingredient is *difficulty*. Difficult goals have a bigger impact on performance than easier goals. It turns out that most people like a bit of a challenge and will put in additional effort. Research suggests that if a person thinks they have a 50/50 shot at success, those odds tend to be maximally motivating. However, if a goal is viewed as unattainable or extremely difficult, it will have the opposite effect on motivation. Why bother trying if you already know you won't succeed? The third ingredient relates to the specific case of teams. *Group-centric goals* (goals designed to maximize individual contributions to team performance) have a significantly bigger impact than *egocentric goals* (goals that are designed around individual accomplishments).

With measurements and improvement goals in place, the next important consideration is how to best support your team's approach to these goals. If you and the team are embarking on something completely new, then a *project management* approach may be most helpful. If, on the other hand, you are looking to make changes to an existing method of doing things, then a *process / quality improvement* approach may be more helpful.

Project Management

Project management involves planning and overseeing a set of activities that lead to a specific end goal, typically along a prespecified timeline. Bigger organizations often manage many large-scale projects at the same time, requiring significant ongoing coordination across them. Sometimes these projects will be coordinated through a project management office. The larger, longer, and costlier a project is within an organization, the more likely it is to be managed using formal project management techniques.

One project management technique that can be particularly helpful, no matter the project size, is a project timeline: a list of specific steps, the individuals responsible for completing them, and their due dates. A timeline can be as simple as a table in a word processor or spreadsheet, with rows identifying the steps that need to be completed. Each row contains a description of the step, followed by the person or persons responsible in the second column, and a due date in the third column. A fourth column can provide space to make notes about current status, and/or a check box to indicate whether the step has been completed.

For more complex projects, leaders often use specialized software packages that help them visualize progress, as well as automate changes to their overall plans (for example, if a step gets delayed by two weeks, the software can automatically move all subsequent steps forward by that amount of time). In recent years, sophisticated project management tools have become available in formats that are much easier to use by people who may not manage projects for a living. Asana and Monday.com are two examples that are popular right now. For less complex initiatives, even simple grids like the one I described earlier can be incredibly helpful communication tools, quickly informing teams about how the projects are progressing and identifying any risks to success.

Process and Quality Improvement

Unlike project management, which focuses on a set of activities with defined start and end points, *process and quality improvement*

(PQI) involves activities that are repeated, with a goal of making them work better over time. PQI processes are central enough to the work of health systems that many adopt specific approaches that they expect all staff to use. Some of the more widespread approaches include A3, Baldrige, DMAIC, Lean, Six Sigma, Lean Six Sigma, Total Quality Improvement, and Toyota Production System. All of these approaches share the following elements: a set of prescribed steps, the use of measures to track progress, and a method for sustaining improvements once they are made. They differ mainly in how each step is described, the terms they use, and the approaches to measurement they favor. At a high level, all models can be described in terms of a cycle of four repeatable phases, as shown in Figure 7.1: *plan, do, study,* and *act.*

In the *plan* phase, the team may first need to spend time coming to agreement about how the current process works. Many aspects of work develop as much out of habits as they do out of an agreed-on set of operating guidelines. Even where clear

7.1 Process and quality improvement cycles

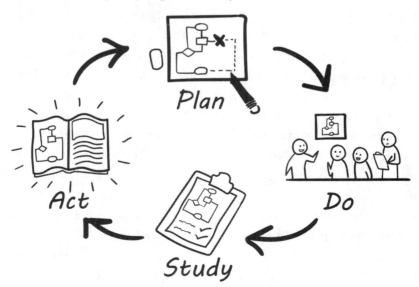

operating guidelines exist, the approaches people take to them may differ wildly from what the guidelines suggest. Visual tools, such as flowcharting, can be particularly helpful in this step of the process.

OK, I realize I promised to keep us out of the weeds, but I do want to spend a little extra time discussing flowcharting. It is a remarkably useful activity, and with a little practice it is very easy to do. Even outside of process improvement efforts, flowcharting can be a very helpful communication tool for helping people quickly understand complicated work processes. At times I have even used flowcharts to check my understanding of how other departments in my organization work, including recruiting, philanthropy, and even how mail gets delivered. I will put something together based on my understanding, give it to my contact in that department, and ask what I got right and wrong. Not only has this exercise been helpful to me directly, but often the person I show the flowchart to asks for a copy they can use to explain to others how their department works.

Now then, back to the plan phase. Once you have the process mapped out, the next steps involve identifying specific changes you may want to make to the process, and then prioritizing which of these potential changes you want to try out. Whenever possible, the best way to prioritize is based on a look at some objective measures, which is why we started the chapter with performance measurement. Measures also allow for a clearheaded examination of potential barriers to specific goals (sometimes called a "root cause analysis"). If more than one potential improvement approach is identified, you may need a method for coming to agreement on which approach to try out first, using methods like those we discussed in the last chapter under "Tying It All Together: Team Leadership."

Once you have identified the improvement approach you want to try out, you then enter the *do* phase. This phase may involve designing a pilot test of the new approach, along with collecting data to evaluate how it went. The *study* phase is when this evaluation takes place, with the results informing how you approach the *act* phase. If things went well, you might agree to keep the approach, making it the new way of doing things. Ensuring this new way of working takes hold could involve creating a new version of your policies (or, even better, your flowchart), teaching the new approach to everyone responsible for the activity, and monitoring the new process to make sure it is implemented consistently.

So there you have it: PDSA. There is, of course, far more that can be learned about process and quality improvement, but this basic framing should provide a solid start. If your organization has adopted a specific approach to process and quality improvement, I definitely recommend getting familiar with it and using it as your primary approach while you are working there. There really isn't a "right" or "wrong" improvement model, and it is usually very helpful for everyone who is working together to share a "common language" of performance improvement.

Strengthening Execution: Learning through Experience

If you are willing to take some initiative, many voluntary leadership opportunities lend themselves particularly well to practicing process and quality improvement. A very well-respected executive recruiter I know once told me the single best way for an early careerist to distinguish oneself when starting a new position is to find some problem that has been bothering everyone and offer to take a crack at making it better. Worst case, the recruiter said, is that you make no progress, and people are still impressed that you were willing to give it a go. Best case is that you make some headway, and you subsequently come to the attention of a lot of important people in the organization. "Who is this new hotshot that just made the impossible happen? And what other impossible problems can she help us figure out?"

If that seems too bold a move for right now, consider instead volunteering to help someone who is doing process improvement work within your organization, or expressing your interests to your manager and seeking their help finding an appropriate project team to join. Most health systems are engaged in process improvement activities all the time, in part because there are so few processes out there that can't be improved upon in seemingly obvious ways. Most are left the way they are because no one has decided that improving them is a high enough priority, but occasionally some find their way to a leader willing to take them on. If you find a good project lead and express an eagerness to learn and contribute, you could help your organization out a lot, and learn quite a bit along the way.

Mentors and Role Models

Although quality improvement is increasingly a required part of clinical professional degrees, having academic exposure does not necessarily make someone an expert in its application. People working within quality improvement departments or who have pursued postgraduate credentials ("black belts" and CPHQ [certified professional in health quality] in particular) may have more practical experience and greater passion to teach what they know. For project management, good mentors can often be found within project management offices and other departments where the work focuses on overseeing longer-term projects (e.g., facilities management). As with quality, there are certifications people can pursue, the best known of which is the PMP (project management professional) from the Project Management Institute (www.pmi.org).

Resources for Learning More

There are several excellent free resource repositories for process and quality improvement in healthcare. The Agency for Healthcare Research and Quality (www.ahrq.gov), a branch of the U.S. Department of Health and Human Services, has a wide variety of free toolkits and guides on its searchable website that are updated continually based on health system needs. The Institute for Healthcare Improvement (www.ihi.org) also offers a breadth of resources on its website, as well as a library of self-paced courses in its Open School. If you are interested in a deeper dive into project management, consider the Introduction to Project Management MOOC from faculty of the University of Adelaide, available on the EDX platform.

CHAPTER 8

Boundary-Spanning

The relations and execution disciplines we explored in the last two chapters focus mainly on people a leader is working with regularly. Successful leadership also involves managing key relationships between this working team and the outside world. These relationships may include, for example, other leaders within a broader organization; external groups responsible for regulation, quality control, and/or monitoring relevant research and innovations; and other organizations providing complementary services within the same communities. In this chapter we will look at how you can develop three particularly important *boundary-spanning* competencies: *relationship and network development, organizational awareness,* and *community collaboration.*

Relationship and Network Development

Effective boundary-spanning involves developing and maintaining new professional relationships. People differ quite a bit in how naturally inclined they are toward these activities. If you are an extrovert, you may enjoy meeting and interacting with people, although your interactions may be more social than strategic. If you are an introvert, you may find that networking drains your energy and that you have to actively resist temptations to leave social events early. Regardless of which description fits you better, there are skills you can practice to become more efficient and effective in your networking activities.

A good starting point is to think about who is important to include in your professional network. In later sections we will consider this question as it relates to people within your own organization (*organizational awareness*) as well as related organizations (*community collaboration*). But first, I want to make sure we discuss the value networking can have for your own growth and development.

From a professional growth perspective, one of the biggest benefits of network development is expanded employment opportunities. Although organizations devote a lot of time and resources to job fairs and online recruiting, most positions are not filled through this discovery process but rather through networking. By some estimates, as many as 80 percent of job openings never even get posted and are instead filled through existing networks (Smith 2013). If this figure seems unbelievably high, I encourage you to talk to a few people further along in their careers about how they found each of their jobs. I am confident the power of networks will quickly become apparent from their responses.

Beyond increasing job prospects, your network can become a very important source of both learning and social support. Let's consider learning first. Regardless of the specifics of your work, there are likely to be many other people out there facing challenges very similar to your own. This was reliably my experience in every collaborative I facilitated for the National Center for Healthcare Leadership, as well as for other organizations. These collaboratives brought together people from different health systems who shared some of the same challenges, typically related to some aspect of organizational learning and change. Time and again, participants in these collaboratives were delighted to learn they were not alone, and they could learn a lot from their peers across the country. There is an old saying that "necessity is the mother of invention," and often the first person to solve a challenge is the one feeling the most pain from it. In a typical group of 15–20 peers, there would be several who had been working especially hard on any challenge they were all facing (e.g., recruiting specific hard-to-find staff, preparing leaders for some emerging challenge, or implementing a productivity application), and who would be further along in solving it than almost anyone else. Usually it meant these pioneers needed to put other challenges on the back burner, and there would be others in the group who were further along than they were on those challenges. The net result was that everyone tended to both "give" and "get" from their participation, and everyone moved forward faster as a result.

Peer sharing of this kind pays another important dividend: social support. Simply knowing that you are not alone in struggling with a particular challenge can help normalize the experience, providing periodic boosts to your self-confidence. Sometimes professional peers can be an even more powerful source of support than friends and significant others, who may not have the same depth of understanding about your lived experiences at work.

Building Your Professional Network: Where to Start

Professional associations can be particularly valuable resources for jump-starting your professional network, if you take the initiative to use them in this way. If you are a clinician (or are studying to become one), there should be at least one association, and likely several associations, offering forums and continuing education opportunities tailored to your profession. The same is true for administrative roles requiring almost any kind of specialized knowledge. Larger associations often have local chapters, providing chances to meet people who know what is going on in your area (including potential future job opportunities).

To get the most out of an association membership, active participation is essential. Associations typically have volunteer opportunities readily available; I encourage you to investigate a few, find one that looks like a particularly good fit for your interests and ability to contribute, and sign up to participate. If multiple opportunities sound interesting, I still recommend starting with just one. Overcommitting to association activities is very easy to do and can run you into trouble down the road. Following through on your commitments is essential for building a strong professional reputation.

How do you identify particularly worthwhile volunteer opportunities? I recommend considering three characteristics closely. The first relates to exposure. Are there other people involved whom you are particularly interested in getting to know? To what extent will the role involve interacting with these people in meaningful ways? The second relates to the associated responsibilities. Try to get a sense of the actual work needs and the extent to which your skills and learning interests are a good match for them. The third is overall time commitment. How long will the role last, and how much time will you be expected to devote during this period? If the role involves participation on a committee, the chair of that committee should be able to readily answer those questions for you, or at least give you reasonable estimates. If they can't, let the chair know what kind of commitment you can make (e.g., "I can comfortably commit to one to two hours a week. Will that be enough time?").

Once you have settled in a bit to your volunteer assignment, find out who the volunteer leaders are and look for an opportunity to introduce yourself to them. Often these individuals have been involved in the association for a while and will be particularly well connected across the membership. If they see that you are making important contributions to the association, they will be motivated to help you. Connecting you with other people is often a very easy way for them to accomplish that.

Making Yourself Discoverable

Managing your online presence is another very important dimension of professional and network development. As your work becomes more visible, people who want to find out more about you will learn what they can from the internet and social media. Currently the most widely used online professional network is LinkedIn. If you creat-e a profile on LinkedIn, people searching for you there will be able to learn about your work and education history, as well as anything else you would like them to know about you professionally. You can also use your LinkedIn profile to connect to other profiles, which many people now find easier than exchanging business cards or other types of contact information. LinkedIn can also be very helpful in learning about someone you may be meeting with in the future, or are interested in getting to know better. I will provide more tips about that in the appendix, which focuses on mentoring. Meanwhile, many of the networking strategies we discussed here are also relevant to the other two competencies in the boundary-spanning discipline, which I will cover next.

Organizational Awareness

Organizational awareness involves understanding the formal and informal structures composing the organization within which you work. Every organization, regardless of size, has both formal and informal structures, and each is important to the organization's work in its own way.

Formal Structures

In chapter 6, I discussed the concept of *legitimized power*, or "power by job description." You can think of the formal structure as essentially the legitimized power structure: the organizationally endorsed relationships of authority between employees. There are three key elements to all formal structures. The first is *work activities*, what needs to be done. In most healthcare organizations, the primary work involves caring for patients; but as we discussed in chapter 4 on health system literacy, patient care requires quite a bit of additional support in areas such as staffing, procuring supplies, and managing information systems and finances. This brings us to the second element: *staff groupings*. As with clinical care, many other aspects of organizational operations run most efficiently and effectively when they are clustered together. The third element is the *reporting structure*. Each employee in an organization will have someone they formally report to. Although reporting relationships can go by different names, *manager* and *direct report* are the most common. Managers are responsible for determining whether each of their direct reports' roles continues to be appropriate for the organization's needs, and also whether the specific direct reports occupying them are the right ones for the work that needs to be completed.

Figure 8.1 depicts a miniature organization chart. Organizations populate these types of charts with names and titles to communicate reporting relationships, particularly within

8.1 Formal organization structure

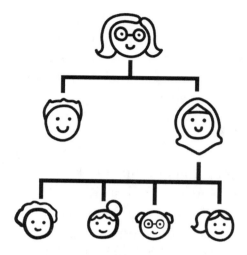

specific subdivisions of organizations. In large organizations, there may be multiple levels of managers reporting up to other managers. This type of hierarchy, sometimes called the *chain of command*, is particularly important for managing tasks and budgets that are too complicated for any one individual to handle on their own. In this case, our figure depicts two levels of management. Another important concept organization charts illustrate is *span of control*, the scope of activity and resources (budget, people, things) for which a given manager is responsible. In our figure, the person on the right wearing a hijab has a span of control of four staff.

Informal Structures

Although the formal structure specifies the ultimate decision-makers in areas such as employment and budget, most day-to-day activity within organizations takes place outside this formal structure, and needs to. *Informal structures*—relationships between people outside the formal hierarchy—form the basis of most work within organizations. Informal structures are estab-

8.2 Informal organization structure

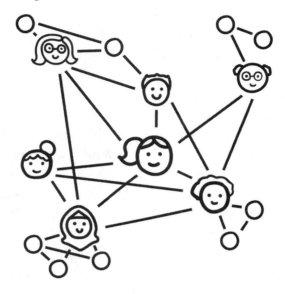

lished over time based on experiences within ongoing working relationships, and although they are more fluid than formal structures, they tend to stabilize over time, taking on specific functional properties.

Figure 8.2 depicts what an informal structure of the same organization might look like. Here the lines between people don't represent a chain of command but rather a set of working relationships. These relationships may involve ongoing collaborative work, or they could involve episodic interactions—for example, someone you might call for help with a specific technical problem, or to learn about what is going on in another department. It is within the informal network that the other sources of power we discussed in chapter 6 are particularly salient.

Expert power is a good example here, and information technology can provide a nice illustration. In many large organizations, if you have a tech problem, you can contact the organization's help desk for assistance. The help desk may assign the problem to support techs on an availability basis; these techs can vary quite a bit in their problem-solving capabilities. Some may be very good at quickly diagnosing what is most likely causing a particular problem, and identifying the best approach to fix it. Others may take more of a "brute force" approach, where they attempt to solve every problem by, for example, wiping the hard drive and rebuilding the operating system. In my own experience, the brute-force approach generally works, but also involves my giving up access to my computer for several days and can require hours of reconfiguration after I get it back. At this late stage in my life, I am highly motivated to seek out the expert problem solvers and avoid the brute-force techs at all costs. Doing so requires learning the names and contact information of the techs who seem to have the most expertise, and finding ways to circumvent the help desk process so that I can contact them directly.

I am hardly the only person who operates this way, nor is information technology the only department where this happens. Across a big organization, there will be many people like me who identify the "stars" in the departments they need to work with, and sidestep the formal hierarchy in order to work with them directly. Over time, if these stars stick around, they often end up becoming important nodes in the informal networks.

Informational power is another important driver of informal networks. Since most organizational activity is based on managing information, finding the right "signals" within all the noise is critically important. Even in organizations committed to transparency, it is very difficult to capture and document everything important going on, and inefficient to wade through all the information sources to find answers to the questions you may be most interested in. It is usually much more efficient to identify knowledgeable people who are more directly involved in activities you need to keep tabs on, and have conversations with them directly.

Informal networks are so important to success that some large organizations have begun mapping them out, analyzing their patterns, and actively shaping them, much as they do their formal networks. Scholars of *social network analysis* have been able to identify common informal network roles, as well as the advantages and challenges often associated with them (Cross and Prusak 2002). *Central connectors*, for example, have the highest number of connections to people across the organization. These individuals often have valuable expertise and/or insights about what is going on across the organization, and are willing to share this knowledge with the people they are connected to. This role tends to be self-reinforcing: as people go to central connectors for their knowledge, they can also become sources of additional knowledge to the connectors. However, every one of these interactions takes time and mental effort, and if the number of connections gets too high it can lead to *collaborative overload*, a sense of being continually behind in managing these relationships, with not enough time in the day to get the core work done. More effective central connectors thus focus on connecting people to others in their network who can help them, rather than trying to help everyone directly. Referrals can offer a similar amount of help in far less time (Cross, Taylor, and Zehner 2018).

Although the focus of our informal networks discussion has been on within-organization relationships, the principles also apply to relationships that span organizations. We turn to this topic next.

Community Collaboration

The missions of health systems typically focus on maintaining or improving health. However, as we discussed in chapter 1, there are very real limits to how much impact any one hospital or clinic can have on people's overall health. The central concept of *community collaboration* involves influencing the "bigger picture" of health overall, beyond what is possible through the care provided by a single organization. These outside influences can relate to, for example, where a person lives, the types of food they eat, their sources of social support, and the stressors they need to manage in their daily life.

Higher-impact approaches to supporting health require complex collaborations. In chapter 1, I described a few examples that hinted at the broader health-related impacts a health system can have beyond clinical care. If you are working for a health system, its senior leaders may already be actively involved in the communities your organization serves in a variety of ways. Your health system may also already be organizing volunteer activities that employees can participate in, and encouraging them to do so. By participating in these types of activities, you are likely to have more impactful contributions on community health.

Although connecting to teams within your organization can create a bigger impact, I definitely would not encourage you to abandon something you are passionate about just because it doesn't seem to be a priority to your coworkers right now. Your unique experiences and perspectives may have given you insights to some paths forward that other people aren't seeing yet. The next chapter, "Transformation," will look more closely at methods for raising awareness and urgency to pursue new and different courses of action. First, however, I want to give you a few ideas about continuing to develop the discipline of boundary-spanning.

Strengthening Boundary-Spanning: Learning through Experience

One of the best ways to develop your boundary-spanning capabilities is by gaining experience bridging your own work to the work and missions of other organizations. A good place to start is by clarifying the professional values that are most important to you, and investigating the ways other types of organizations can influence the greater good those values represent. For example, if you are a respiratory therapist (or conditions such as asthma are particularly important to you), consider looking for environmental justice organizations in your area that are working on the root causes of local air pollution. Your expertise and leadership capabilities could help them move their work forward, and their advocacy could in turn help your patients and others you care about. Alternatively, maybe you have observed other general challenges to maintaining health and well-being in the patients your organization serves, or in your own lived experience, such as access to transportation, unhealthy living conditions, or commitments to others that crowd out self-care. Pick the challenge you are most passionate about, and find out who else is working to address it, or would like to be.

Mentors and Role Models

Most health systems are already engaging with their communities through departments (or "offices") with names like community relations, community services, and/or community health. In your HR department there may also be people focused on community hiring, apprenticeships, and other work-based learning programs. The people who are engaged in leading and/or championing these types of activities are often terrific role models and potential mentors for boundary-spanning. They may also be able to help you identify groups and organizations with the biggest needs for your skills and passion for the causes you care about most.

Resources for Learning More

In addition to the many professional associations working on boundary-spanning activities, there are some terrific organizations focused specifically on helping health systems pursue greater impact through community collaborations. One of the most impressive I am familiar with is the Healthcare Anchor Network (HAN; www.healthcareanchor.network). The HAN is closely aligned with the anchor institution concept from chapter 2 and gets its support from organizational membership dues and charitable grants. The network regularly puts together insightful resource guides that are available for anyone to download for free from its website. The Association for Community Health Improvement (ACHI; www.healthycommunities.org) is another good source of information about community engagement. ACHI is part of the American Hospital Association and receives support from individual memberships, conference programs, and corporate sponsorships. Its website also contains a number of valuable resources, including a comprehensive community engagement "toolkit."

If you are particularly passionate about environmental sustainability, there are many online resources available to help health systems support these efforts. The largest and most established is Health Care Without Harm (www.noharm.org), and its associated organizational membership program, Practice Greenhealth (www.practicegreenhealth.org). Both websites contain many helpful resources that are freely available to the public. At the time of this writing, more than one third of U.S. hospitals were Practice Greenhealth members. If you work for a health system that is a member, you can e-mail the organization to find out who your representative is, and this individual can help connect you to sustainability work that may already be going on within your organization.

CHAPTER 9

Transformation

If you want to truly understand something, try to change it.
—*Kurt Lewin*

The final leadership discipline, *transformation*, focuses on how leaders can successfully pursue systemic change. Unlike the process and quality improvement approaches described in chapter 7, *transformation* is not about tweaking existing processes; it is about fundamental redesign. If incremental changes will do, then quality improvement approaches should be used. But if it is clear that current approaches to things will not be successful in the future, then bigger changes are called for.

Of all the disciplines we discussed in this book, transformation tends to be the most difficult. Attempting to change an entrenched organizational system can make the day-to-day challenges of leadership seem like a walk in the park. While the other disciplines—execution, relations, and boundary-spanning—can all help with transformation, each is more of an entry ticket than a ticket to success. This chapter will build on the previous ones by introducing several competencies that are particularly helpful to systems transformation: *strategic orientation, innovative thinking,* and *change leadership.*

Seeing What's Coming: Strategic Orientation

Organizational systems all share a characteristic that is at once their greatest strength and their greatest vulnerability: *inertia,* a strong tendency to keep things going exactly as they have been. As people become more experienced in their organizational roles, more of their work becomes habit, interactions become more predictable, and everything tends to operate more efficiently and with less drama. All of these qualities are strengths for doing the day-to-day work. They are also why changes to these stable systems can feel so disruptive. The quicker and more urgent the change, the more stress will be experienced. Conversely, with more advanced notice about emerging needs for change, people can have a greater sense of control over the future, rather than feeling like a victim of circumstances.

Strategic orientation involves scanning the internal and external environments on an ongoing basis for changes that may affect your work in the future, and using what you learn to consider potential opportunities and threats. An important goal of strategic orientation is to give yourself and the people you work with a longer lead time in preparing for these necessary adaptations. Another important goal is to clarify which environmental changes merit immediate attention, which ones you may just want to keep an eye on for now, and which ones you can safely ignore for the foreseeable future.

How can you strengthen your strategic orientation? The author William Gibson gives us a clue in this quote: "The future is already here, it's just not very evenly distributed" (Quote Investigator, n.d.). Most changes unfold as part of the cyclical patterns described in the previous chapters, and even though they can sometimes seem sudden, most often they trace back to much smaller changes that began long ago. If you learn how and where to look for them, these hints about what's to come—sometimes called *signals* (Institute for the Future, n.d.)—can create a clearer picture of what the future may hold.

For interested readers, appendix 2 provides specific suggestions about sources of signals. For now, I mainly want to stress that finding signals is as much about your mindset as it is about specific sources. The widely respected futurist Jane McGonigal has said her favorite place to find signals is on Google, simply by searching on "the future of ____" and replacing the blank with whatever she is most interested in (McGonigal, n.d.). Although a single search of this type is unlikely to provide a clear roadmap of the future, if you develop the habit of doing these types of searches over time, you will start to train yourself to call out the more meaningful signals from the less meaningful ones.

Transforming Systems: Change Leadership

Unlike quality improvement initiatives, organizational changes involve a more discernible beginning, middle, and end. But as with quality improvement, organizations often adopt a specific change model that they encourage everyone to use. If your organization has such a model, I recommend learning about it and adopting it if you can. In case your organization does not have a model, or if the model seems incomplete or otherwise problematic, I will suggest a terrific one for you. It was authored by John Kotter (2012) and is described in much greater detail in

9.1 Phases of organizational change

Preparing for change	Implementing change	Sustaining change
• *Sense of urgency* • *Guiding coalition* • *Vision development*	• *Communicating vision* • *Empowering action* • *Short-term wins*	• *Consolidating gains* • *Anchoring to culture*

his many books, of which *Leading Change* is his most widely known. The Kotter model includes eight steps, which can be pursued sequentially but generally require some circling back and forth along the way. I find it helpful to divide the steps into three broad phases, as illustrated in figure 9.1: preparing, implementing, and sustaining.

Preparing for Change

Before describing the first phase, I want to share several critically important observations about transformational change. First, it is almost always anxiety-provoking, and at times downright terrifying. Second, it generally only happens if it *must*—in other words, only if *not* changing seems even scarier and more inconceivable than the transformation at hand. Change leaders sometimes describe this dynamic as the "burning platform," which gets its name from the real-life *Piper Alpha* oil rig explosion in 1988. The explosion, which took place off the east coast of Scotland, set ablaze both the oil rig itself and the oil-covered water 300 feet below. Most of the rig's crew died in the disaster, but one of the survivors, a superintendent, lived to describe his harrowing escape. Upon being awakened by the explosion and subsequent alarms, he made his way out to the edge of the platform, where he saw, some 15 stories below, burning oil and twisted debris all across the water's surface. Were he to survive a plunge into the water, the best he could hope for was 20 minutes of life before he would succumb to hypothermia. Should he take his chances on the rig? Or risk a potentially fatal jump for the possibility of buying himself a little extra time to be rescued? We only know this story because he did jump, and as a result was rescued. In the end, the choice between jumping and staying was a choice between his probable death and his certain death (Conner 2012).

Thankfully, most transformational change efforts don't involve putting people's lives in jeopardy. But for success, Kotter (2012) argues, they all require a *sense of urgency*. My own experience over many decades concurs: if a change effort doesn't feel sufficiently urgent, it is doomed to be abandoned as soon as something that seems more urgent comes along. The pattern has been so consistent that I now regularly decline invitations to participate in change efforts (those I have a choice to decline, anyway) if I don't think the urgency is adequate. I have also abandoned initiatives I was leading in their early days for the same reason. Choosing carefully means I have a lot more energy available for the ones I believe have a genuine shot at success.

Assuming a sense of urgency has been clearly established, the next step involves bringing together a *guiding coalition*, the right people to carry the change process forward. Once this group is together, the next step involves developing a *vision* for the change process and a *strategy* for how to engage people with it.

I want to draw attention to an important point here: the first three stages of Kotter's eight-stage model (a little over a third of them) happen before any of the real implementation work even starts. In real life, I see many change efforts try to skip one or more of these first three stages. I then usually see the effort go off the rails later. As with the team stages from chapter 6, the temptation is to move to action before people are on the same page as to what the action should be, resulting in more "storming" down the road.

Implementing Change

Ideally, leaders begin the implementation phase by systematically *communicating the change vision*. The goal in this step is to educate everyone who will be involved in the change process about why the change is so important, what it's going to involve, and what roles each of them may need to take in it. At this stage, the change process becomes real to people, and so does resistance to it. Although each individual response is unique in some ways, they can all be usefully categorized based on two scales, as illustrated by figure 9.2: type of response (positive to negative) and level of involvement (high to low). *Champions* of the change process have a more positive response and greater eagerness to be directly involved in supporting the change effort's success. *Helpers* also have a positive response but are less involved than champions. *Bystanders*, in contrast, have a neutral or possibly more negative response

9.2 Responses to an organizational change (individual differences)

but do not actively interfere with the change effort. The last category is *resisters*, those who generally stand to lose the most from the change and may actively attempt to prevent its success.

Supporting and empowering champions is a critically important role for the change leaders and the guiding coalition. Inevitably, champions and resisters will butt heads along the way. Resisters frequently cite current policies, structures, and resource constraints as reasons why the various steps in the change process can't happen. A particularly popular resister phrase is "We can't do that because ____," the blank filled in with all manner of glass-half-empty ideas: lack of training ("we don't know how"), lack of resources ("we can't afford it," "we don't have time"), or lack of authority ("we need vice president approval"). Champions will need help finding paths around these roadblocks; the job of the change leader and the guiding coalition is to help create those paths. For larger change efforts within larger organizations, this help may involve moving people temporarily into new positions to help with the change process. It may also involve enrolling people in just-in-time training programs or providing new productivity and communication tools. Or it could involve being an alternative source of "permission" to do the things that their immediate bosses are telling them they can't do, such as directly approving new hires or other expenses needed to support the change effort.

Supporting champions also involves cheering them on periodically, which brings us to the next step: *generating short-term wins*. At this point you may be getting a sense that the transformational change process can become a bit of a slog. The champion, who is being helped out by leadership, is probably not getting a cheerful response from the resisters they are circumventing. Quite the opposite. The resisters, more worried now, may be stepping up their efforts to sabotage forward progress. Or they may still be biding their time, betting that this change effort will eventually implode as others have in the past. In either case, milestones—opportunities for visible progress—are very important for keeping hope alive.

According to Kotter (2012), effective short-term wins have three properties. First, they are widely visible. Ideally, they don't require a change champion to be on hand pointing them out or explaining them; anyone can see them for themselves. Second, they are clear in signaling progress, offering little or no opportunity for debate. Third, they are explicitly tied to the change effort at hand. Goals that were publicly set at the start of the change process are a particularly good example, especially if people were initially skeptical about their success.

Sustaining Change

Once a change effort has begun to pay off, the natural response for change leaders is to start relaxing a bit. Psychologically, there can be a sense that a finish line has been crossed and victory is at hand. Ironically, this very sense of success can mean the change effort is entering a period of renewed vulnerability. This is true in part because people are so good at dealing with short-term crises. When our adrenaline is pumping, it helps us focus our attention, learn new things quickly, rapidly develop new ways of relating to others, and monitor their effects. And once the perceived crisis has passed, we are equally good at returning to business as usual, which typically means falling back on our longer-term, more deeply ingrained, nonconscious habits, also called our "comfort zone."

Making transformational changes stick requires not only learning new approaches but also unlearning old ones. This typically involves practicing the new approaches long enough for them to become our new comfort zone. The last two steps in Kotter's model describe this process. In *consolidating gains*, the focus shifts toward making some of the temporary structures permanent. For example, shortcuts and temporary work-arounds orig-inally created to help champions of change get things done could be turned into permanent approaches to the work going forward. Similarly, some temporary reassignments made to support the change effort may be turned into permanent roles. The final step, *anchoring to the culture*, involves changing the organization's ap-proaches to how staff are hired, on-boarded, rewarded, and re-directed so that the changes become understood as the way to do things going forward.

Opportunities and Threats: Understanding Individual Reactions to Organizational Change

As plans for organizational change are crafted, it is important to consider the effects they will have on people. These effects are never evenly distributed. Inevitably, organizational changes af-fect some more than others, both in terms of how much the changes require of them personally and in terms of the gains and losses they experience. Some of these effects can be anticipated, and more sensitively managed, using an understanding of the ways people tend to experience emotional threats. The SCARF model, developed by David Rock (2009), is a particularly useful framework for analyzing the potential impact of change initia-tives, based on known neurological bases of threat response.

SCARF is an acronym for five perceived threats that are salient to organizational change (see figure 9.3). The first threat, to *status*, involves a person's relative sense of standing within the organ-ization. Changes involving a person's title, work location, or other publicly visible sources of identity are likely to carry meaning for their perception of status. The second threat, to *certainty*, relates to how predictable a person perceives their environment to be. When faced with ambiguity, we naturally tend to seek out expla-nations or come up with our own, a process sometimes referred

9.3 Threat reactions to change: The SCARF model

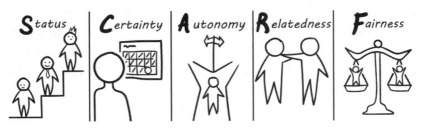

to as "sensemaking." Communicating regularly and consistently about what to expect in a change process can go a long way toward restoring a greater sense of certainty. The third threat is to *autonomy,* one's sense of personal control in their work. To the extent that a change process involves telling people to do their work differently, it will diminish their sense of autonomy. While to some degree this impact is unavoidable, involving people as much as possible in decisions that will ultimately affect them can help preserve their sense of autonomy. Drawing attention to aspects of the work that are still under their discretion can also be helpful.

The fourth threat, to *relatedness,* involves how changes may affect current working relationships. For example, moving individuals to different teams or outside the organization typically creates a sense of loss among the remaining people who had been working with them. Working with new and unfamiliar people is usually also a source of stress, at least until a baseline level of trust and predictability is developed. Leaders can help manage these responses by acknowledging the difficulties these changes create and by providing forums where people can talk through some of their experiences with the changes. When new working relationships need to be forged, investing time early on in establishing norms can help people work together more quickly.

The final threat is to *fairness,* the extent to which people feel they are being treated equitably in relation to their coworkers.

People are most resilient to changes, especially those involving personal losses, if they believe the process that led there was similar for everyone they work with. In fact, all else being equal, people will generally prefer a worse outcome over a better one, if the worse outcome was fair and the better one was not (Tabibnia and Lieberman 2007). For people to view a change process as fair, they generally need to feel they understand how decisions are being made. Regular communications about the "what" and the "why" of change are very important, as are opportunities to ask additional questions and voice concerns. For changes taking place across larger organizations, senior leaders may give managers specific "talking points" on a regular basis to discuss with their teams. Managers may also be instructed to ask team members for questions and feedback, which they then compile and send on to senior leadership so that reactions can be monitored across the organization.

Strengthening Transformation: Learning through Experience

The best way to learn about transformation is through participation. Advocacy efforts and volunteer roles in community-based organizations can offer these types of opportunities. Although the specific challenges may differ, many of the interpersonal dynamics discussed throughout the chapter are consistent across settings. If you want to develop a robust mental model of change from all sides, consider seeking out different change activities in which you assume each of the main roles we discussed: champion, helper, bystander, and, yes, even resister (since sometimes the most just course of action involves getting in the way). Participating in each of these roles will deepen your self-awareness and better prepare you to work with others across these roles in the future.

Mentors and Role Models

The best way to sort out who is an effective change agent and who is less so is through their accomplishments over time. In general, people who are new to an organization seem like more effective change agents than they do a few months down the road, owing to a "honeymoon" effect of sorts. People who have been with an organization longer, and have been able to move more substantial changes forward without losing their jobs in the process, can make for particularly good mentors. Change leadership in general lends itself well to mentoring, because most change leadership efforts are readily converted into "change stories," which can be enjoyable and at times even therapeutic for leaders to talk about. If you find someone who has found success by applying a specific change model, their experiences can be especially valuable. Such experiences and stories lend themselves much better to the retelling, and they are much more likely to be broadly applicable than the "I made it up as I went" method. There are also people who specialize in change management professionally, and associations and credentials catering to them. The most widely recognized of these is the Association of Change Management Professionals (www.acmp.org), and the Certified Change Management Professional (CCMP) credential.

Resources for Learning More

Earlier I mentioned the work of John Kotter. His book *Leading Change* is a classic in the field and remains almost as engaging and applicable as when it first came out in the 1990s. You can find a copy at many local libraries and in the business section of most used bookstores. Kotter's more recent book *Accelerate (XLR8)* expands on his original concepts and applies them specifically to informal change networks within organizations.

Conclusion

You are not a drop in the ocean. You are the entire ocean in a drop.
—*Rumi*

When I first started my healthcare career some 30-plus years ago, I was part of the final generation to grow up before the dawn of the World Wide Web, social media, and smartphones. Absent these tools, clear roles and hierarchies were our most dependable guides for getting work done in organizations. Both made clear who should think of themselves as leaders, and who as followers.

Ever since that time, the value of hierarchies in organizations has continued to fade. Today, they function less like pillars for keeping a building upright, and more like roadmaps for organizing collective decision-making. Leadership, too, is less tied up in positions and even individuals, and is becoming more like water, flowing in harmony with changes to the shape of the organizations containing it.

Looking ahead, many current trends hint that health systems could rise to more prominent roles in building a better future. Indeed, given both their size and their health-related missions, they may have little choice. And they will need help—lots of it—from everyone involved, you included.

My goal in writing this book is to equip you to contribute to this brighter future. In chapter 2 on accelerating your own leadership development, I described how leadership expertise is acquired foremost through practice, good feedback, open-minded reflection, and more practice. In the chapters that followed, on the seven disciplines, I brought together the most valuable, practical, and evidence-based leadership lessons I could fit in a book of this size. I now invite you to go out there and lead. Healthcare needs you. As does our future.

Developing Mentoring Relationships

I n chapter 2 on accelerating leadership development, I describe the essential role of high-quality feedback; in the chapters on the seven disciplines, I suggest places to look for good role models and mentors. In this appendix I will give you some tips on engaging people to become mentors, and suggestions on how to make the most of these important relationships. For our purposes, I define *mentor* as anyone other than your boss who is willing to voluntarily provide you with some level of ongoing support, guidance, and/or advice that may help you develop your leadership capabilities.

If you have read the earlier chapters, the benefits of mentors should already be clear. But you may still be wondering why someone would volunteer their time to mentor you, particularly if they already seem quite busy. It's true that mentoring is not for everyone. For that matter, not everyone is good at mentoring, at least not right from the start. But lots of people truly enjoy mentoring, and, as with every other leadership skill, they can get better at it over time, with practice and feedback. There are other payoffs for mentors as well: they tend to have greater job satisfaction, higher organizational commitment, and quicker career success than their colleagues who don't mentor (Ghosh and Reio 2013). Mentors also often find this role very professionally fulfilling, especially if protégés (mentees) manage their side of the relationship well.

Approaching a Potential Mentor

Before asking someone to mentor you, first make sure you are clear about what you want out of the relationship, as well as what you are willing to put into it. For example, are you looking for guidance on career decisions, or help with a specific leadership discipline? If the latter, which one? Are you hoping for a few meetings over a short period of time, or a longer-term relationship, perhaps involving an annual check-in or two in the years to come? Sometimes informal relationships work best; however, if you are hoping for a longer-term commitment, working out a more specific agreement may make sense. A good approach can involve structuring your "ask" along the following lines: (1) stating your goals, (2) explaining why you are reaching out to them specifically, and (3) making a specific initial request. Here's an example:

> I am reaching out to you today because I am working on getting better at leading organizational changes. I was given your name by _____, who said you are the most effective change agent they have ever worked with. Would you be willing to meet with me sometime, at your convenience, so I could ask you some questions about your work?

Pause for a moment now, and consider how you might react to a request like this one. If you're like most people, you'd be flattered, and would be enticed by the chance for more such compliments. Or, you might feel you don't have time for this meeting, but the message itself would not have been experienced as a nuisance. If you do get a decline on your invitation, you can make a more modest follow-up request for a nomination of someone else this person thinks would be good to approach. Continuing to build your professional network in this way is almost always time well spent.

Your First Meeting

Once a potential mentor has agreed to an initial meeting, make it easy for them to participate. Ask for their guidance on the best way to schedule with them (e.g., do they have someone who manages their calendar?), and the best time of the day and week for them. Offer to come to their office or meet in another location convenient for them. If you can afford to, consider offering to take them to breakfast or lunch at a favorite restaurant.

In getting ready for this first meeting, take as much personal responsibility as you can for ensuring its success. Prepare an agenda of the topics you'd like to cover, and a good set of questions to ask. Make sure you arrive early, and stay conscious of time during the meeting itself. Bring something to do in case they are running late, and be understanding if they are. Let them know when you are running toward the end of the allotted time so that you don't inadvertently make them late for their next appointment—but be willing to stay longer if the conversation is going well and they have additional time they'd like to share with you.

As you are wrapping up the meeting, mentally ask yourself how things went. If you thought they went well and you'd like to continue the working relationship, then after you thank them for their time, ask if they might be willing to meet up again periodically in the future. If they say yes, you have found yourself a mentor.

Managing Your Mentoring Relationship

The best mindset to have about mentors is that they are a valuable resource in short supply, and you are fortunate to have found one. It is a good idea to reinforce this perspective each time you meet with your mentor. In addition, it never hurts to convey that you want to be as helpful to them as they are being to you—if not now, then at some point in the future. Another way to reinforce this mindset is indirectly, through how wisely you use the working relationship and your time together.

Managing Mentoring Meetings

However many demands you may have on your time, your mentor's schedule may be even tighter, so do your best to set meetings for times when there is no risk that you will have to reschedule. As a meeting draws near, make sure you prepare carefully so that your time together is used most wisely. No matter how informal your conversations may be, it is always a good idea to have an agenda in your own mind.

If you have set development goals for yourself, now is a good time to review them, making note of any successes, lessons learned, and questions they may suggest for discussion. If you implemented any of your mentor's advice from your last meeting, be sure to note that as well. Next, consider any upcoming events or activities where your mentor's input could be helpful. Finally, try to identify any topics or areas that provide you with an opportunity to give back. For example, if you have run across any articles or videos on topics of interest to your mentor, you can offer to send them along if she confirms they are of interest. For all of the above, I recommend making notes along the way so that you remember everything you'd like to discuss.

Using Time in between Meetings

Before you end a meeting, try to identify at least one specific "homework assignment" you can make progress on before your next meeting. Doing so will help you stay accountable to making the most of the learning relationship. The "assignment" can be as simple as applying a specific piece of advice you received from your mentor, and keeping track of how things went. This will help you mark progress, and also tee up your next conversation. You may even find your mentor starts to look forward to hearing the outcome of your next "chapter," making for an even more engaging mentoring relationship.

Build in Periodic Reviews

Although your mentor may be willing to set up a relationship that is open ended, setting a specific time frame has many advantages, particularly in terms of keeping a clear focus. Along the same lines, agreeing to periodic reflections about how the working relationship is going can help you take stock of progress and also decide when to end the formal part of the relationship. For example, if you asked your mentor to work with you because of her strengths in a particular discipline, the two of you may evaluate your progress and decide if you have made the progress you had hoped to. You may then make an intentional decision to either wrap up the meetings or perhaps continue them with a different focus. Without this type of structure, the mentoring relationship may simply taper off over time, which is usually a less satisfying way to leave things.

End the Formal Relationship Well

If you have followed the time frame suggestions above, I recommend scheduling a wrap-up conversation that you both understand will be your final formal meeting. At this meeting, you can express your gratitude for the progress your mentor helped you make. Even after the mentoring relationship has formally ended, plan to check in periodically to keep the relationship going. For example, you could set a calendar reminder to send an e-mail a year or so after your final meeting. In it you can give an update on your work and career, mentioning any ways that their work with you has been especially helpful, and also ask about how their work has been going.

Developing a Longer-Term Mindset

Foresight Resources and Strategies

> The most important question we must ask ourselves is,
> "Are we being good ancestors?"
> —*Jonas Salk*

When you think about what the future may hold, how far into the future do you imagine? If you are like most people, your time horizon does not extend very far. Recent research suggests that more than a quarter of U.S. adults rarely or never think about their lives even five years ahead, and more than half never consider life 30 or more years from now (Institute for the Future 2017). This short-term bias, which was critical to survival throughout most of human history, has become more of a collective liability than an asset. In recent decades especially, many of the biggest threats needing our attention—in society and in our environment—move too slowly to be noticed in the present; they can only be seen and fully understood at the time-scale of human generations. Successfully addressing these challenges will require us to sustain much longer-term courses of action, something our societies are not yet well designed for. Even among the leaders of large enterprises, attention tends to be bound within financial reporting cycles—a coming month, quarter, or fiscal year. When longer-term planning does get discussed, it is often defined on a time horizon of just three to five years. Rarely are an organization's activities or impacts considered in the context of decades, let alone generations.

In this appendix, I offer some strategies for expanding the time horizons of your own thinking, and of the people you work with. I will also provide examples of methods that foresight practitioners (sometimes called "futurists") use to help people envision potential future states, to inspire more meaningful dialogue about these longer time horizons. In doing so, I hope to heighten your interest in long-term thinking and equip you to help others understand what their own short-term actions look like through the lens of long-term impact.

Starting with You: Personalizing a Time Horizon

One of the most compelling ways to think about a distant point in the future is to create a vision of yourself at that mile marker. To get an even clearer sense of how things evolve over longer periods, mentally travel backward in time by that same amount. For example, if you are interested in what some aspect of the world may look like in 10 years, consider first what you think your own life will look like. How old will you be? Where do you imagine you will be working? How might your age have affected your day-to-day life, and those of your loved ones? If you do the same exercise in reverse, you can ask similar questions: How old were you 10 years ago? Where were you then, and what were you doing? How were you physically different? And how was the world different?

If you are trying to help others develop a longer-term perspective, a decade can be a useful time frame to work with on an exercise like this one. Even younger adults can typically remember what life was like when they were in their early teens, and will also be able to identify specific ways in which the world has changed since then. However, in the context of our contemporary challenges—equity and ecological sustainability, in particular—a decade may still not be long enough to reveal the shape of these trends, and a timescale that spans generations may be needed. Let's say we want to think about the world 50 years from now. Or 100. Looking backward, constructing a longer-term perspective may require a review of written histories or documentaries, and getting perspectives from the generations before you if you can. Looking forward, developing this longer-term perspective may require looking through the lens of an extended family. For example, if you don't think you will still be here 50 years from now, you could apply the questions above to your current or future children, nieces and nephews, or those of your friends or neighbors.

Projecting Forward from Long-Term Trends

Organized systems of all kinds tend to operate according to inertia: trends toward growth tend to continue growing, trends of decline tend to continue declining, and systems in equilibrium tend to stay that way. However, some systems are more robust to outside influence than others. The futurist Daniel Burrus (2017) refers to more robust trends as *hard trends*. Like freight trains, hard trends tend to speed along in their current direction until they crash into something bigger than they are, at which point the inertia meets resistance and the trend begins to slow down.

Human population is a good example of a hard trend. We can make a darn good guess about how many 18-year-olds there will be in the world 17 years from now, given that they were all already born. Even beyond this rather obvious example, demographers have found they can make pretty accurate assessments of the population growth we are likely to see in the future, even over very long periods of time (National Research Council 2000). As with other species, when human subpopulations have crashed in the past, it was usually because the population began depleting local resources—arable soil, animals, and water, in particular—at a faster pace than they could be replenished. By measuring the upper limits of resources (also called *carrying capacity*), the end point of local population growth can also be forecast pretty accurately. Once that limit is reached, either new resources must be found or the population must level off or decline. Biology dictates it.

Similar principles hold true for organizations. Left to their own devices, they take on the characteristics of the economic systems within which they operate, such that survival demands continued expansion over time. The rate of this growth almost inevitably exceeds growth in the underlying market (the organization's resource base), leading first to competition between organizations, then to consolidation among them (Grullon, Larkin, and Michaely 2019). Surviving organizations then extend the growth pattern for a time by continuing to evolve their goods and services beyond what customers have asked for and continuing to demand higher prices for them. That strategy meets its end when new organizations learn to give customers what they actually wanted in the first place at inevitably lower costs—a process that has been called *disruptive innovation* (Christensen 2003). If the dominant organizations are powerful enough, they may choose to prevent these new organizations' success (e.g., by funding the creation of new regulatory barriers), or they may simply buy the new organizations as they spring up. But if these new organizations are successful enough fast enough, they will continue to chip away at the old organizations' markets until these newcomers prevail, and the cycle will start all over again.

While hard trends can help you understand the likely range of potential future states, combining them into a coherent whole can quickly become a mind-numbingly complex task. Intersections between the trends often don't point in one definitive direction, but rather toward several plausible ones. Add to this our own perceptual biases, and you can quickly find yourself feeling as though you are walking around in a circle. Similar to walking around without a map, even when you find insights along the way, you may find it difficult to explain them so that other people understand how you got there. For all of these reasons, a step-by-step analysis framework can be very helpful.

Putting It All Together: Developing an Analysis Framework

To develop a clearer and more conveyable perspective about the future, you first need to identify a focal point for your analysis. A good approach is to thoughtfully fill in the blank: "The future of ___." If you are working on this perspective as part of a team, consider asking people to fill in the blank independently, and then compare responses. The end goal is for the statement to be broad enough that you will be able to find a good amount of source material to inform it, and narrow enough that specific implications for action can be identified. Getting there may involve iterating through several drafts.

Once you have identified your focal point, the next step is to prepare a framework for synthesizing the information sources that will inform it. For this step I will usually create a grid, with space in the first columns to identify information sources and the people who will review them, followed by important categories of trend information in the subsequent columns. While there is no one correct set of categories to use for every application, there are several sets frequently used for this type of analysis. One is STEEP: social, technology, economic, environmental, and political. Another is PESTLE: political, economic, social, technical, and legal. Later in this appendix I will provide a visual example of such a grid.

When I am conducting this type of review, I typically start with one of these category sets, and add or replace categories to align more tightly with the focal point at hand. For topics related to healthcare, I might include, for example, culture of health, higher education, health professions, health systems, and work/workforce. The end result will look something like the column headers in figure A2.1.

Identifying Good Source Material

In addition to describing trends as relatively hard or soft, sources can also be described in terms of how hard (objective) or soft (subjective) they seem to be. Relatively objective sources involve measurable data; they are less prone to human biases but also require more interpretation. Relatively subjective sources rely more on human analysis and interpretation. Subjective sources may offer a much more vivid picture of potential futures; however, they also need to be interpreted with some caution, and ideally with some understanding of the author's background and professional agenda. Rather than sug-

A2.1 Example foresight project matrix

Sources		Trend Categories									
Source	Reviewer Initials	Demographics	Education	Energy/ environment	Geopolitical	Health culture	Health systems	Health professions	Socio-economic	Technology	Work/ Workforce
Source #1						X	X			X	
Source #2			X						X		X
Source #3						X	X				
Source #4			X						X		X
Source #5						X	X			X	
Source #6		X	X	X			X		X		
Source #7		X									
Source #8		X		X	X					X	
Source #9								X			
Source #10		X	X	X	X	X	X		X	X	X

gesting one source is better than others, I generally recommend identifying a variety of source types and then looking for common themes across them.

At the end of this appendix I provide examples of objective and subjective sources that I have found useful. It is not a comprehensive list, and I encourage you to supplement it by identifying some favorites of your own. If your work on a foresight project involves other people, I also recommend involving team members in identifying sources to inform this step of the analysis. Doing so can widen the scope and diversity of sources in useful ways, and create a much greater sense of collective ownership of the results. It's OK if a few sources are less credible or more controversial, as long as they are counterbalanced by a good number of more objective sources, and your analysis focuses on patterns across them.

Review and Synthesis

If you have pulled together a good amount of raw material for review, you will next need a process for distilling this material down to a manageable summary. When completing this step, I will typically create a grid like the one in figure A2.1 in a virtual space that facilitates simultaneous editing (e.g., Google sheets, Microsoft Teams). In the first column I will list all of the sources we plan to review; column two will list the individuals who have agreed to review each of them. Subsequent columns will list topical categories we are most interested in informing. As we review each source, we will make note of any specific predictions the source describes, and which category or categories they relate to. I refer to these as "future facts" and will place a sequential number under the appropriate column or columns to provide citation numbers for later use. In a separate word processing document, I will summarize each future fact in narrative form in the section corresponding to that category, along with the appropriate number to reference the source. This approach allows all future facts to be clustered together and reviewed as a package later on.

Once the initial sources have been reviewed, the next step is to look at the overall distribution of future facts across categories. Often the results will be lopsided: some categories may have too many future facts and will need further distilling; others may have too few. Make note of any category that either has very few future facts or was derived from a much smaller number of sources than the others. From there, you can first revisit how important the category is to the task at hand. If you believe the category is indeed very important, seek out additional sources to round it out. If you still come up empty-handed, note this as a set of findings you need to be more tentative about.

Once the review has been completed, the next step involves synthesizing the results into a more readily digestible format. The goal in this step is to create one or more perspectives about the future that feel unfamiliar enough to push your audience to think, but also plausible enough that they are not simply dismissed out of hand. Of the many methods out there for creating a synthesis, I have found two that are particularly compelling. The first, and best known, is to use *scenarios*, fictional descriptions of several potential future states. A commonly used approach involves creating several scenarios based on different levels of optimism and pessimism. For example, one scenario might ask what the future may hold if everything possible goes right, another might involve everything going wrong, and a third might trace forward business-as-usual. I have seen scenarios work particularly well in situations where they can help people decide between moving in a new strategic direction and staying on the current course or, to borrow a phrase from chapter 9, visualizing a burning platform.

The second method, *personas*, involves creating descriptions of what one or more individuals' lives might look like in the future.

Personas are often developed as part of a user-centered design approach and can be equally effective for creating a more vivid perspective of the future (Fergnani 2019). For a health system setting, a persona might embody one or more major groups of patients (or customers) you work with today, as envisioned in the future time period you have chosen. A persona might alternatively embody the people who will work for your organization in the future. A well-crafted persona should ideally give people a way to relate to your perspective of the future on a more intimate level. Personal details such as a name, age, occupation, and family can be very helpful, as can stock photographs depicting the persona. In addition to creating this general structure for the persona's life, it is important to flesh out an emotional side—for example, what are the persona's aspirations? What barriers are they experiencing to achieving them, and what are they doing to overcome them? What are they most worried about, and what steps are they taking to keep those concerns under control?

Putting Foresight to Use

Analyses and exercises like these are only useful if they meaningfully influence perspectives and decision-making. Ideally, scenarios and personas should be routinely reviewed during strategic planning, becoming a consistent and early step in these deliberations. Incorporating them can be as simple as pausing the process to ask and discuss: "What will this plan look like if Scenario A is our future?" "What about Scenario B?" "How would this approach affect Persona A?" "How about Persona B?"

In addition to organizational strategic planning, these techniques can also inform individual and departmental decision-making. New hires are an excellent example. In healthcare settings especially, staff often feel stretched very thin, and when someone leaves an organization, the hiring manager may feel pressured to fill the open role very quickly. It can be tempting to simply recruit someone similar to the person who just left the job. But a better first step is to consider where the team may be going in the years to come—for example: What new skills might the team need several years from now? What other transitions (e.g., departures, promotions, new hire opportunities) may unfold during this period? With a clearer sense of what the team could look like in the future, a hiring manager can then more thoughtfully consider whether a new hire, at the present time, and into the role as currently envisioned, is truly the ideal path forward—versus, for example, distributing responsibilities within the current team, automating or outsourcing portions of the role, promoting someone internally into the role, and/or reallocating the resources to create a different type of position.

Resources for Learning More

Data Sources

In figure A2.2 I provide a list of sources I have found particularly valuable for exploring long-term trends. Many of these sources have freely downloadable datasets, allowing you to explore the various ways long-term cycles may interact with one another. Several also offer free visualization tools on their sites.

Analysis Frameworks

If you are interested in learning more about the scenario planning process, the American Planning Association has a publicly searchable knowledge base on this topic, with links to many sources that are available for free on the web (www.planning.org /knowledgecenter/). There are also several nonprofit organizations that periodically develop scenarios relevant to health and healthcare for public use; these include the Institute for Alternative Futures (2014), Institute for the Future (2016), and the

A2.2 Exploring long-term trends: Sources for U.S. and global trend data

Category	Topic	Source	Description
(All)	(All)	Our World in Data[i]	Datasets and graphs for a very wide range of relevant domains; authoritative, well referenced and accessible
Climate change		Global Climate Change (NASA)[ii]	Trend data and graphs on carbon atmospheric levels, 800,000 years ago to present, benchmarked to 1950 levels
		U.S. Environmental Protection Agency (EPA)[iii]	Trend databases on greenhouse gas emissions, overall and by industry
		Intergovernmental Panel on Climate Change (IPCC)[iv]	Graphs and datasets for carbon atmospheric projections out 80+ years, using different sets of assumptions
Consumer finances	Household finances	U.S. Census Bureau[v]	Data on a breadth of household finance topics including housing costs, commuting habits
	Consumer debt	Federal Reserve Bank of NY, Center for Microeconomic data[vi]	15-year trends and graphs, as well as historical data, in categories such as student loans, home loans, auto loans, and credit cards
	Inflation	U.S. Bureau of Labor Statistics, Consumer Price Index[vii]	Data and interactive charts / search tools over 40 years. Also searchable by location and specific consumer items.
	Healthcare costs	Centers for Medicare & Medicaid Services—National Health Expenditure Data[viii]	Historical datasets on healthcare costs starting in 1960
	Healthcare costs	Kaiser Family Foundation[ix]	Databases and interactive trend graphs starting in 1999; emphasizes costs to individuals
	Higher education costs	U.S. Department of Higher Education / NCES[x]	Data tables for 30+ years, as well as reports spanning 100+ years
	Poverty rates	U.S. Census Bureau[xi]	Historical datasets from 1959 to 2018 describing poverty rates, overall and by a variety of family and other demographic groups

Demographics	(All)	U.S. Census Bureau [xii]	Projections by age group, gender, ethnicity, and citizenship for up to 40 years
Employment	(All)	Bureau of Labor Statistics [xiii]	Ten-year projections of growth by job category
Environment/ pollution	Carrying capacity	Global Footprint Network [xiv]	Ecological footprint biocapacity time series graphs starting in 1961 up to 2016
	Plastics/ microplastics	Our World in Data [xv]	Data visualizations and downloadable datasets charting historical and projected (30-year) waste volumes
Human health	(All)	CDC - National Center for Health Statistics [xvi]	Datasets and visualizations on a breadth of health topics spanning multiple decades

[i] https://ourworldindata.org/
[ii] https://climate.nasa.gov/evidence/
[iii] https://www.epa.gov/
[iv] http://www.ipcc-data.org/
[v] https://www.census.gov/data.html
[vi] https://www.newyorkfed.org/microeconomics/hhdc.html
[vii] https://www.bls.gov/cpi/
[viii] https://healthdata.gov/
[ix] http://www.kff.org
[x] https://nces.ed.gov/fastfacts/
[xi] https://www.census.gov/data/tables/time-series/demo/income-poverty/historical-poverty-people.html
[xii] https://www.census.gov/data.html
[xiii] https://www.bls.gov/emp/
[xiv] https://www.footprintnetwork.org/licenses/
[xv] https://ourworldindata.org/plastic-pollution
[xvi] https://www.cdc.gov/nchs/data-visualization/

World Economic Forum (Walker 2016). If you would like to learn more about the use of personas, I encourage you to check out the "Personas" page on the Usability.gov website (https://www .usability.gov/how-to-and-tools/methods/personas.html). Although the site's focus is user experience design rather than foresight, most principles are directly applicable to both.

Bibliography

Adler-Milstein, Julia, Carol E. Green, and David W Bates. 2013. "A Survey Analysis Suggests That Electronic Health Records Will Yield Revenue Gains for Some Practices and Losses for Many." *Health Affairs* 32 (3): 562–570.

Agha, Leila. 2014. "The Effects of Health Information Technology on the Costs and Quality of Medical Care." *Journal of Health Economics* 34:19–30.

AHA Community Health Improvement. 2020. "Community Health Assessment Toolkit." July 31, 2020. https://www.healthycommunities .org/resources/community-health-assessment-toolkit.

Alghamadi, Ahlam, Aryn C. Karpinski, Andrew Lepp, and Jacob Barkley. 2020. "Online and Face-to-Face Classroom Multitasking and Academic Performance: Moderated Mediation with Self-Efficacy for Self-Regulated Learning and Gender." *Computers in Human Behavior* 102:214–222.

American Planning Association. n.d. "Knowledgebase Collection: Scenario Planning." Accessed July 30, 2020. https://planning.org /knowledgebase/scenarioplanning/.

Ames, Daniel, Lily Benjamin Maissen, and Joel Brockner. 2012. "The Role of Listening in Interpersonal Influence." *Journal of Research in Personality* 46:345–349.

Association for Community Health Improvement. n.d. *Community Health Assessment Toolkit: Community Engagement.* Accessed February 20, 2021. https://www.healthycommunities.org/resources/toolkit /files/community-engagement.

Asurion. 2019. "Americans Check Their Phones 96 Times a Day." Cision, November 21, 2019. https://www.prnewswire.com/news-releases /americans-check-their-phones-96-times-a-day-300962643.html.

Batty, Michael, Christa Gibbs, and Benedic Ippolito. 2018. "Unlike Medical Spending, Medical Bills in Collections Decrease with Patients' Age." *Health Affairs* 37 (8): 1257–1264.

Becker's. n.d. *13 Statistics on Hospital Profit and Revenue in 2011.* Accessed June 30, 2020. https://www.beckershospitalreview.com/finance/13 -statistics-on-hospital-profit-and-revenue-in-2011.html.

Bernard, Diane. 2020. "Three Decades before Coronavirus, Anthony Fauci Took Heat from AIDS Protestors." *Washington Post*, May 20, 2020. https://www.washingtonpost.com/history/2020/05/20/fauci -aids-nih-coronavirus/.

Bessen, James. 2015. "Toil and Technology." International Monetary Fund, March 2015. https://www.imf.org/external/pubs/ft/fandd /2015/03/bessen.htm.

Bischoff, Paul. 2020. "172 Ransomware Attacks on US Healthcare Organizations since 2016 (costing over $157 million)." Comparitech, February 11, 2020. https://www.comparitech.com/blog/information -security/ransomware-attacks-hospitals-data/.

Bock, Laslo. 2015. *Work Rules! Insights from inside Google That Will Transform How You Live and Lead.* New York: Twelve.

Bowen, H. R. 1955. "Business Management: A Profession?" *Annals of the American Academy of Political and Social Science* 297:112–117.

Boyatzis, Richard. n.d. "Inspiring Leadership through Emotional Intelligence." Accessed February 21, 2021. https://www.coursera.org /learn/emotional-intelligence-leadership.

Brown, Brené. 2018. *Dare to Lead: Brave Work. Tough Conversations. Whole Hearts.* New York: Random House.

Burke, Brian L., Andy Martens, and Erik H. Faucher. 2010. "Two Decades of Terror Management Theory: A Meta-Analysis of Mortality Salience Research." *Personality and Social Psychology Review* 14 (2): 155–195.

Burrus, Daniel. 2017. *The Anticipatory Organization.* Austin, TX: Greenleaf Book Group Press.

Cameron, Kim S., and Robert E. Quinn. 2011. *Diagnosing and Changing Organizational Culture* (3rd ed.). San Francisco: Jossey-Bass.

Campbell, W. Keith, and Constantine Sedikides. 1999. "Self-Threat Magnifies the Self-Serving Bias: A Meta-Analytic Integration." *Review of General Psychology* 3 (1): 23–43.

Castro, Dotan R., Frederik Anseel, Avraham N. Kluger, Karina J. Lloyd, and Yaara Turjeman-Levi. 2018. "Mere Listening Effect on Creativity and the Mediating Role of Psychological Safety." *Psychology of Aesthetics, Creativity, and the Arts* 12 (4): 489–502.

CBS Interactive. 2019. "Hackers Are Stealing Millions of Medical Records—and Selling Them on the Dark Web." February 14, 2019. https://www.cbsnews.com/news/hackers-steal-medical-records-sell -them-on-dark-web/.

Centers for Medicare & Medicaid Services. n.d. *NHE Summary, Including Share of GDP, CY 1960–2018 (ZIP).* Accessed August 18, 2020. https:// www.cms.gov/files/zip/nhe-summary-including-share-gdp-cy-1960 -2018.zip.

Cheeseman, Jennifer, and Andrew W. Hait. 2019. "Number of Truckers at All-Time High." United States Census Bureau, June 6, 2019. https://www.census.gov/library/stories/2019/06/america-keeps-on -trucking.html.

Christensen, Clayton. 2003. *The Innovator's Solution: Creating and Sustaining Successful Growth.* Boston: Harvard Business Review Press.

Collini, Stevie A., Ashley M. Guidroz, and Lisa M. Perez. 2013. "Turnover in Health Care: The Mediating Effects of Employee Engagement." *Journal of Nursing Management* 23 (2): 169–178.

Conner, Daryl. 2012. "The Real Story of the Burning Platform." Conner Partners, August 15, 2012. https://www.connerpartners.com /frameworks-and-processes/the-real-story-of-the-burning-platform.

Courtright, John A., and Scott E. Caplan. 2020. "Two Meta-Analyses of Mobile Phone Use and Presence." *Human Communication & Technology* 1 (2): 20–35.

Cowan, Jill. 2020. "What's Different about the Protests in Los Angeles This Time." *New York Times,* June 3, 2020. https://www.nytimes.com /2020/06/03/us/los-angeles-george-floyd-protests.html.

Cross, Rob, and Laurence Prusak. 2002. "The People Who Make Organizations Go—or Stop." *Harvard Business Review,* June, 104–112.

Cross, Rob, Scott Taylor, and Deb Zehner. 2018. "Collaboration without Burnout." *Harvard Business Review,* July–August, 134–137.

Daly, Rich. 2019. "Hospitals Innovate to Control Labor Costs." Healthcare Financial Management Association, October 1, 2019. https://

www.hfma.org/topics/hfm/2019/october/hospitals-innovate-to
-control-labor-costs.html.

Diener, E. 2009. "Assessing Subjective Well-Being: Progress and Opportunities." In *Assessing Well-Being: The Collected Works of Ed Diener*,
25–65. New York: Springer.

Dye, Carson F., and Andrew N. Garman. 2015. *Exceptional Leadership:
16 Critical Competencies for Healthcare Executives* (2nd ed.). Chicago:
Health Administration Press.

Dyer, W. Gibb, Jr., Jeffrey H. Dyer, and William G. Dyer. 2013. *Team
Building: Proven Strategies for Improving Team Performance* (5th ed.). San
Francisco: Jossey-Bass.

Dyrbye, Lisolette N., Colin P. West, Daniel Satele, Sonja Boone, Litjen
Tan, Jeff Sloan, and Tait D. Shanafelt. 2014. "Burnout among U.S.
Medical Students, Residents, and Early Career Physicians Relative
to the General U.S. Population." *Academic Medicine* 89 (3): 443–451.

EDX. n.d. "Introduction to Project Management." Accessed February 21,
2021. https://www.edx.org/course/introduction-to-project
-management.

Epton, Tracy, Sinead Currie, and Christopher J. Armitage. 2017. "Unique
Effects of Setting Goals on Behavior Change: Systematic Review and
Meta-Analysis." *Journal of Consulting and Clinical Psychology* 85 (12):
1182–1198.

Ericsson, K. Anders, Ralf Th. Krampe, and Clemens Tesch-Romer. 1993.
"The Role of Deliberate Practice in the Acquisition of Expert
Performance." *Psychological Review* 100 (3): 363–406.

Erikson, David, Ian Galloway, and Naomi Cytron. 2012. "Routinizing
the Extraordinary." In *Investing in What Works for America's Communities: Essays on People, Place, & Purpose*, 377–406. San Francisco: Federal
Reserve Bank of San Francisco and Low Income Investment Fund.

Fergnani, Alessandro. 2019. "The Future Persona: A Futures Method to
Let Your Scenarios Come to Life." *Foresight* 21 (4): 445–466.

Fisher, Roger, William L. Ury, and Bruce Patton. 2011. *Getting to Yes:
Negotiating Agreement Without Giving In* (3rd ed.). New York: Penguin
Books.

Fleenor, John W., James W. Smither, Leanne E. Atwater, Phillip W. Braddy, and Rachel E. Sturm. 2010. "Self-Other Agreement in Leadership: A Review." *Leadership Quarterly* 21:1005–1034.

French, J. P., and B. Raven. 1959. "The Bases of Social Power." In *Studies in Social Power*, edited by D. Cartwright, 150–167. New York: Institute for Social Research.

Garman, Andrew N., Melanie P. Standish, and Joyce Anne Wainio. 2020. "Bridging Worldviews: Toward a Common Model of Leadership across the Health Professions." *Health Care Management Review* 45 (4): E45–E55.

Gates, Bill. 1996. *The Road Ahead.* New York: Penguin Books.

Ghosh, Rajashi, and Thomas G. Reio Jr. 2013. "Career Benefits Associated with Mentoring for Mentors: A Meta-Analysis." *Journal of Vocational Behavior* 83:106–116.

Google. n.d. "Our Mission." Accessed February 21, 2021. https://about.google.

Gosling, Samuel D. 2020. "Two Short Measures of Values (TIVI and TWIVI)." GozLab, August 11, 2020. https://gosling.psy.utexas.edu/two-short-measures-of-values-tivi-and-twivi/.

Green, Paul, Francesca Gino, and Bradley Staats. 2017. "Shopping for Confirmation: How Disconfirming Feedback Shapes Social Networks." Working Paper, Harvard Business School, Cambridge, MA. https://hbswk.hbs.edu/item/shopping-for-confirmation-how-disconfirming-feedback-shapes-social-networks.

Greenberg, Jeff, Tom Pyszczynski, and Sheldon Solomon. 1986. "The Causes and Consequences of a Need for Self-Esteem: A Terror Management Theory." In *The Public and Private Self*, edited by Roy F. Baumeister, 189–212. New York: Springer.

Grullon, Gustavo, Yelena Larkin, and Roni Michaely. 2019. "Are US Industries Becoming More Concentrated?" *Review of Finance* 23 (4): 697–743.

Hall, Mary N. 2016. "Power Is Not a Dirty Word." *Family Medicine* 48 (3): 236–237.

Harkin, Benjamin, Thomas L. Webb, Betty P. I. Chang, Andrew Prestwich, Mark Conner, Ian Kellar, Yael Benn, and Paschal Sheeran. 2016. "Does Monitoring Goal Progress Promote Goal Attainment? A

Meta-Analysis of the Experimental Evidence." *Psychological Bulletin* 142 (2): 198–229.

Hart, William, Dolores Albarracin, Alice H. Eagley, Inge Brechan, Matthew J. Lindberg, and Lisa Merrill. 2009. "Feeling Validated vs. Being Correct: A Meta-Analysis of Selective Exposure to Information." *Psychological Bulletin* 135 (4): 555–588.

Hillestad, Richard, James Bigelow, Anthony Bower, Federico Girosi, Robin Meili, Richard Scoville, and Roger Taylor. 2005. "Can Electronic Medical Record Systems Transform Health Care? Potential Health Benefits, Savings, and Costs." *Health Affairs* 24 (5): 1103–1117.

Himmelstein, David U., Terry Campbell, and Steffie Woolhandler. 2020. "Healthcare Administrative Costs in the United States and Canada, 2017." *Annals of Internal Medicine* 172 (2): 134–143.

HIMSS. 2014. *25th Annual HIMSS Leadership Survey.* Research Report, HIMSS. http://s3.amazonaws.com/rdcms-himss/files/production /public/FileDownloads/2014-HIMSS-Leadership-Survey.pdf.

———. 2019. *2019 HIMSS Cybersecurity Survey.* Survey research report, HIMSS. https://www.himss.org/sites/hde/files/d7/u132196/2019 _HIMSS_Cybersecurity_Survey_Final_Report.pdf.

HIV.gov. n.d. "A Timeline of HIV and AIDS." Accessed August 23, 2020. https://www.hiv.gov/hiv-basics/overview/history/hiv-and-aids -timeline.

Hoff, Kevin A., Daniel A. Briley, Colin J. M. Wee, and James Rounds. 2018. "Normative Changes in Interests from Adolescence to Adulthood: A Meta-Analysis of Longitudinal Studies." *Psychological Bulletin* 144 (4): 426–451.

Hood, C. M., K. P. Gennuso, G. R. Swain, and B. B. Caitlin. 2016. "County Health Rankings: Relationships between Determinant Factors and Health Outcomes." *American Journal of Preventive Medicine* 50 (2): 129–135.

Initiative for a Competitive Inner City. 2002. *Leveraging Colleges and Universities for Urban Economic Revitalization: An Action Agenda.* https://icic.org/wp-content/uploads/2016/04/ICIC_Leveraging -Colleges.pdf.

Institute for Alternative Futures. 2014. "Public Health 2030: A Scenario Exploration." May 1, 2014. https://kresge.org/sites/default/files /Institute-for-Alternative-Futures-Public-Health-2030.pdf.

Institute for the Future. 2016. "Caregiving 2031." June 30, 2016. https://www.iftf.org/caregiving2031/.

——. 2017. *The American Future Gap*. Research report. https://www.iftf.org/fileadmin/user_upload/downloads/IFTF_TheAmericanFutureGap_Survey_SR-1948.pdf.

——. n.d. "Signals." Accessed February 21, 2021. https://www.iftf.org/what-we-do/foresight-tools/signals/.

Jiaxin, Yang, Xi Fu, Liao Xiaoli, and Li Yamin. 2020. "Association of Problematic Smartphone Use with Poor Sleep Quality, Depression, and Anxiety: A Meta-Analysis." *Psychiatry Research* 284:1–9.

Johansen, Bob. 2017. *The New Leadership Literacies: Thriving in a Future of Extreme Disruption and Distributed Everything*. Oakland, CA: Berrett-Koehler.

Jones, Damon, David Molitor, and Julian Reif. 2019. "What Do Workplace Wellness Programs Do? Evidence from the Illinois Workplace Wellness Study." *Quarterly Journal of Economics* 134 (4): 1747–1791.

Kane, Robert L., Matthew Maciejewski, and Michael Finch. 1997. "The Relationship of Patient Satisfaction with Care and Clinical Outcomes." *Medical Care* 35 (7): 714–730.

Keehan, Sean P. 2020. "National Health Expenditure Projections, 2019–2028: Expected Rebound in Prices Drives Rising Spending Growth." *Health Affairs* 39 (4): 704–714.

Klaus, Peggy. 2003. *Brag! The Art of Tooting Your Own Horn without Blowing It*. New York: Warner Business Books.

Kleingeld, Ad, Heleen van Mierlo, and Lidia Arends. 2011. "The Effect of Goal Setting on Group Performance: A Meta-Analysis." *Journal of Applied Psychology* 96 (6): 1289–1304.

Kluwer, Avraham N., and Angelo DeNisi. 1996. "The Effects of Feedback Interventions on Performance: A Historical View, a Meta-Analysis, and a Preliminary Feedback Intervention Theory." *Psychological Bulletin* 119 (2): 254–284.

Koranne, Rahul. 2020. "Healthcare Delivery Providers." Coursera, August 6, 2020. https://www.coursera.org/learn/healthcare-delivery-providers.

Kotter, John P. 2012. *Leading Change*. Boston: Harvard Business School Press.

———. 2014. *Accelerate: Building Strategic Agility for a Faster-Moving World.* Boston: Harvard Business School Press.

Kottke, Thomas E., Matt Stiefel, and Nicolaas P. Pronk. 2016. "'Well-Being in All Policies': Promoting Cross-Sectoral Collaboration to Improve People's Lives." *Preventing Chronic Disease* 13. https://www .cdc.gov/pcd/issues/2016/16_0155.htm.

Lilly, Meredith B., Audrey Laporte, and Peter C. Coyte. 2007. "Labor Market Work and Home Care's Unpaid Caregivers: A Systematic Review of Labor Force Participation Rates, Predictors of Labor Market Withdrawal, and Hours of Work." *Milbank Quarterly* 85 (4): 641–690.

McGonigal, Jane. n.d. "Where Do You Look for Signals? And Other FAQ." Coursera. Accessed July 30, 2020. https://www.coursera.org /lecture/introduction-to-futures-thinking/where-do-you-look-for -signals-and-other-faq-mxm5j.

Medina, Jennifer. 2017. "The L.A. Riots 25 Years Later: A Return to the Epicenter." *New York Times*, April 28, 2017. https://www.nytimes.com /2017/04/28/us/la-riots-rodney-king-south-central-1992.html.

Millenson, Michael M. 2018. *Half a Century of the Health Care Crisis (and Still Going Strong).* HealthAffairs, September 12, 2018. https://www .healthaffairs.org/do/10.1377/hblog20180904.457305/full/.

Morris, Zoe Slote, Steven Wooding, and Jonathan Grant. 2011. "The Answer Is 17 Years, What Is the Question: Understanding Time Lags in Translational Research." *Journal of the Royal Society of Medicine* 104 (12): 510–520.

Moyo, Mpatisi, Felicity A. Goodyear-Smith, Jennifer Weller, Gillian Robb, and Boaz Shulruf. 2016. "Healthcare Practitioners' Personal and Professional Values." *Advances in Health Science Education* 21:257–286.

Mullen, B. 1983. "Egocentric Bias in Estimates of Consensus." *Journal of Social Psychology* 121:31–38.

National Academies of Sciences, Engineering, and Medicine. 2019. *Taking Action against Clinician Burnout: A Systems Approach to Professional Well-Being.* Washington, DC: National Academies Press. nam .edu/ClinicianWellBeingStudy.

National Center for O*NET Development. n.d. "My Next Move." Accessed August 1, 2020. https://www.mynextmove.org/explore/ip.

National Research Council. 2000. *Beyond Six Billion: Forecasting the World's Population*. Washington, DC: National Academies Press.

Patterson, Kerry, Joseph Grenny, Ron McMillan, and Al Switzler. 2012. *Crucial Conversations: Tools for Talking When the Stakes Are High*. New York: McGraw-Hill.

Peterson, D. R. 1976. "Is Psychology a Profession?" *American Psychologist* 31 (8): 572–581.

Pollitz, Karen, Cynthia Cox, and Rachel Fehr. 2019. "Claims Denials and Appeals in ACA Marketplace Plans." KFF. February 25, 2019. https://www.kff.org/health-reform/issue-brief/claims-denials-and-appeals-in-aca-marketplace-plans/.

Quote Investigator. n.d. "The Future Has Arrived—It's Just Not Evenly Distributed Yet." Accessed February 21, 2021. https://quoteinvestigator.com/2012/01/24/future-has-arrived/.

Rock, David. 2009. "Managing with the Brain in Mind." *Strategy + Business*, August 27, 2009, 1–10. https://www.strategy-business.com/article/09306?gko=9efb2.

Roser, Max, Estaban Ortiz-Ospina, and Hannah Ritchie. 2019. "Life Expectancy." Our World in Data, October 1, 2019. https://ourworldindata.org/life-expectancy#life-expectancy-has-improved-globally.

Rush University Medical Center. 2016. "Rush Community Health Needs Assessment Report." https://www.rush.edu/sites/default/files/2020-09/rush-chna-august-2016%284%29.PDF.

Salas, Renee N., Edward Maibach, David Pencheon, Nick Watts, and Howard Frumkin. 2020. "A Pathway to Net Zero Emissions for Healthcare." *BMJ* 371:1–11. doi:10.1136/bmj.m3785.

Sastry, Anjuli, and Karen Grigsby Bates. 2017. "When LA Erupted in Anger: A Look Back at the Rodney King Riots." NPR, April 26, 2017. https://www.npr.org/2017/04/26/524744989/when-la-erupted-in-anger-a-look-back-at-the-rodney-king-riots.

Schencker, Lisa. 2019. "Hackers Target Health Data: 82% of Hospital Tech Experts Reported 'Significant Security Incident' in Last Year." *Chicago Tribune*, March 8, 2019. https://www.chicagotribune.com/business/ct-biz-hospital-data-breaches-20190307-story.html.

Schwartz, Shalom H. 1992. "Universals in the Content and Structure of Values: Theoretical Advances and Empirical Tests in 20 Countries." *Advances in Experimental Social Psychology* 25:1–65.

———. 2012. "An Overview of the Schwartz Theory of Basic Values."
Online Readings in Psychology and Culture 2 (1). doi:https://doi.org/10
.9707/2307-0919.1116.

Seehausen, Maria, Philipp Kazzer, Malek Bajbouj, and Kristin Prehn.
2012. "Effects of Empathic Paraphrasing—Extrinsic Motivation
Regulation in Social Conflict." *Frontiers in Psychology* 3:1–11.

Shanafelt, Tait, Joel Goh, and Christine Sinsky. 2017. "The Business
Case for Investing in Physician Well-Being." *JAMA Internal Medicine*
177 (12): 1826–1832.

Shuck, Brad. 2011. "Four Emerging Perspectives of Employee Engagement: An Integrative Literature Review." *Human Resource Development
Review* 10 (3): 304–328.

Sitzmann, Traci, Katherine Ely, Kenneth G. Brown, and Kristina N.
Bauer. 2010. "Self-Assessment of Knowledge: A Cognitive Learning
or Affective Measure?" *Academy of Management Learning & Education*
9 (2): 169–191.

Smith, Jacquelyn. 2013. "7 Things You Probably Didn't Know about
Your Job Search." *Forbes*, April 17, 2013. https://www.forbes.com/sites
/jacquelynsmith/2013/04/17/7-things-you-probably-didnt-know
-about-your-job-search/.

Solomon, Sheldon, Jeff Greenberg, and Tom Pyszszynski. 2015. *The
Worm at the Core: On the Role of Death in Life*. New York: Penguin
Random House.

Starr, P. 1982. *The Social Transformation of American Medicine*. New York:
Basic Books.

Stavrinos, Despina, Caitlin N. Pope, Jaibin Shen, and David C.
Schwebel. 2018. "Distracted Walking, Bicycling, and Driving:
Systematic Review and Meta-Analysis of Mobile Technology and
Youth Crash Risk." *Child Development* 89 (1): 118–128.

Susskind, Richard E., and Daniel Susskind. 2015. *The Future of the
Professions: How Technology Will Transform the Work of Human Experts*.
Oxford: Oxford University Press.

Suzuki, Severn. n.d. "Speech at U.N. Conference on Environment and
Development." Accessed August 30, 2020. https://www.american
rhetoric.com/speeches/severnsuzukiunearthsummit.htm.

Tabibnia, Golnaz, and Matthew D. Lieberman. 2007. "Fairness and
Cooperation Are Rewarding: Evidence from Social Cognitive

Neuroscience." *Annals of the New York Academy of Science* 1118(1): 90–101.

Tuckman, Bruce W. 1965. "Developmental Sequence in Small Groups." *Psychological Bulletin* 63 (6): 384–399.

Usability.gov. n.d. "Personas." Accessed July 1, 2020. https://www.usability.gov/how-to-and-tools/methods/personas.html.

U.S. Bureau of Labor Statistics. n.d. "CPI Inflation Calculator." Accessed August 16, 2020. https://www.bls.gov/data/inflation_calculator.htm.

U.S. Centers for Disease Control and Prevention. 1986. "Current Trends Update: Acquired Immunodeficiency Syndrome—United States." January 17, 1986. https://www.cdc.gov/mmwr/preview/mmwrhtml/00000667.htm.

———. n.d. "Well-Being Concepts." Accessed July 12, 2020. https://www.cdc.gov/hrqol/wellbeing.htm.

Walker, Melanie. 2016. "Healthcare in 2030: Goodbye Hospital, Hello Home-spital." November 11, 2016. https://www.weforum.org/agenda/2016/11/healthcare-in-2030-goodbye-hospital-hello-home-spital/.

Wallace-Wells, David. 2019. *The Uninhabitable Earth: Life after Warming.* New York: Tim Duggan Books.

Ward, Adrian F., Kristen Duke, Ayelet Gneezy, and Maarten W. Bos. 2017. "Brain Drain: The Mere Presence of One's Own Smartphone Reduces Available Cognitive Capacity." *Journal of Applied Communication Research* 2 (2): 140–154.

Watts, Nick et al. 2021. "The 2020 Report of the Lancet Countdown on Health and Climate Change: Responding to Converging Crises." *Lancet* 397 (10269): P129–170. doi:https://doi.org/10.1016/S0140-6736(20)32290-X.

West, C. P., L. N. Dyrbye, and T. D. Shanafelt. 2018. "Physician Burnout: Contributors, Consequences, and Solutions." *Journal of Internal Medicine* 283:516–529.

White, Kenneth R., and John R. Griffith. 2019. *The Well-Managed Healthcare Organization.* Chicago: Health Administration Press.

Wilson, Timothy D., and Elizabeth W. Dunn. 2004. "Self-Knowledge: Its Limits, Value, and Potential for Improvement." *Annual Review of Psychology* 55:493–518.

Woo, Tiffany, Roger Ho, Arthur Tang, and Wilson Tam. 2020. "Global Prevalence of Burnout Symptoms among Nurses: A Systematic Review and Meta-Analysis." *Journal of Psychiatric Research* 123:9–20.

World Health Organization. 2020. "About Social Determinants of Health." Accessed July 1, 2020. https://www.who.int/social _determinants/sdh_definition/en/#:~:text=The%20social%20 determinants%20of%20health,global%2C%20national%20and%20 local%20levels.

———. n.d. "Constitution." Accessed July 29, 2020. https://www.who.int /about/who-we-are/constitution.

Wright, Ronald. 2005. *A Short History of Progress.* New York: Carroll & Graf.

Acknowledgments

The contents of this book were assembled after more than 30 years of reflecting on leadership and healthcare. The contents were shaped by so many generous and thoughtful people that I cannot possibly fully acknowledge all of them here. Even if I could, many of the most important insights I received over the years came from mentors who generously let me believe their ideas were somehow my own. So I will begin by expressing my gratitude for every person who lent me a hand along the way just because it struck them as the right thing to do. To all of those mentors, I hope in reading this book you recognize some of the contributions you made to my development, as I attempt to faithfully pass them along to others.

With that expressed, there are also many people who had memorable and direct impacts in shaping this book, as well as my decision to write it. My immediate family was my first crucible for understanding interpersonal dynamics, and laid the foundation for my personal and professional values. I am grateful to have Robert Garman as a father, a wonderful role model of kindness, open-mindedness, hard work, and a willingness to take thoughtful chances. My mother Carolyne, a teacher of English as a second language, gave me a firm grounding in language, an appreciation for education, and connection to others. I thank my older brother Ray for going first into the world and letting me learn from his experiences, and my Aunt Betty Robinson for being such a kind-hearted and optimistic role model for social change. My college years at Penn State laid the foundation for how I would think about professional and social responsibility; I absorbed many important perspectives from people connected to the peer counseling programs that Sharon Mortenson led, and a particularly patient college counselor named Earl Merritt, who helped me find my way to majoring in psychology. The Virginia Consortium Program gave me my first real exposure to health systems, and how pivotal their roles were in supporting clinicians' abilities to help their patients. In my early days as a clinical psychologist, I was given the chance to work on leadership projects full time at the University of Chicago by Pat Corrigan, an important mentor in my formative professional years, along with his colleagues Tom D'Aunno and Stan McCracken. During this time I discovered the Society of Consulting Psychology, whose members provided particularly impactful mentoring, including one, Dick Kilburg, whose sage counsel helped me through many difficult times in my professional career. When I decided to return to school, Roya Ayman at the Illinois Institute of Technology was instrumental in creating a path that allowed this to happen, and the faculty across their industrial/organizational psychology department have been invaluable collaborators ever since.

Academia is one of the few contexts where ideas can go to battle without fear of harming the people behind them. During my tenure at Rush, I have had the benefit of learning from literally hundreds of practitioner faculty, and facilitating the learning of hundreds more in classrooms and workshop settings. Keeping in touch with them over the years helped me clarify what really matters in leadership roles. I have been blessed to work with supportive department chairs, who themselves were outstanding leadership role models. My good friend and former boss, Peter Butler, tops this list, and continues to have a profound impact on my understanding of leadership. My current and prior core faculty colleagues Jeff Canar, Jerry Glandon, Dan Gentry, Diane Howard, Tricia Johnson, Chien-Ching Li, Denise Oleske, and Shital Shah continue to inform and enrich my understanding of leadership. Beyond the core faculty, I have had the benefit of learning from many of Rush's leaders who are involved with our organization's anchor mission work, racial justice action committee, sustainability, and/or leadership development initiatives, including John Andrews, Brandon Ciarlo, Sheila Dugan, Nina Dutta, Melinda Earle, George Fitchett, Angela Freeman, Diane Gallagher, Carmel Gaughan, Nicole Gilson, Darlene Hightower, Ian Hughes, Michael Jones, Sue Lawler, Mary Nash, Kurt Olson, Christopher Nolan, Patti O'Neil, Rahul Patwari, Terry Peterson, Janet Shlaes, Alita Tucker, and Shweta Ubhayakar. Much of this book is informed by the practical wisdom they have so generously shared with me. The leadership experiences and perspectives of the many facilitators and collaborators in leadership courses I taught have also been important sources for this work, which have included Ross Abrams, Casey Brackett, Mitch Cooper, Susan Crown, Mike Dandorph, Armen Gallucci, Larry Goodman, Robert Higgins, Courtney Kammer, Ranga Krishnan, Omar Lateef, David Leach, Jim Rice, Paula Wilson, and Liz Wurth.

Beyond Rush, the work described in this book benefited from a breadth of scholarly collaborations and thought partnerships spanning decades. One of the most substantive has been with Carson Dye, who I co authored my very first book with, and continue to work with to this day. My colleagues at the Academy of Management, American College of Healthcare Executives, Association of University Programs in Health Administration, and Commission on Accreditation of Healthcare Management Education have provided both direct support and a thriving professional learning community for decades. This includes collaborations with my colleagues Matt Anderson, Sue Boren,

Lihua Dishman, Michael Harrison, John Lloyd, Daniel Kim, Ann McAlearney, Katherine Meese, Larry Prybil, Julie Robbins, Margaret Schulte, Paula Song, Anthony Stanowski, and Larry Tyler, among a great many other kindred spirits. Early on, Errol Biggs was instrumental in my involvement with the University of Colorado executive program, providing another essential window into leadership across the healthcare sector—a relationship the program's new director, Rulon Stacey, has graciously continued. For almost a decade, I have had the good fortune of working with and learning from the National Center for Healthcare Leadership's board, staff, and communities of practice. The very existence of this opportunity was because of the groundbreaking work of Gail Warden, the organization's founder, and Marie Sinioris, the prior CEO, as well as the outstanding work of Joyce Anne Wainio, vice president of operations. I also benefited tremendously from a long and productive working relationship with Tim Rice, a former clinician as well as a health system CEO, who provided essential formative feedback to early drafts of this work. His successor in the role, Jill Schweiters, was also an important inspiration in developing a perspective that leadership is becoming increasingly important at all levels in healthcare. Christy Lemak has been a particularly important collaborator in this role, as have the leads of NCHL's groundbreaking initiatives over the years, including Cassia Carter, Jarrett Fowler, Alia Ibrahim, Callie Lambert, Nitasha Kassam, Marie Rowland, Melanie Standish, and Lindsey Tucker.

The influential participants in the National Center for Healthcare Leadership's learning communities over the years are also too numerous to identify, but I will call out at least a few. Many members of the Leadership Excellence Networks' steering committee have been particularly impactful on my thinking, including Diane Adams, Patty Adelman, Eric Bacigal, Joe Cabral, Gina Cronin, Aimee Daily, Chris Newell, Sue Recko, Maura Walden,

Tara Weideman, Ted Witherell, and Michael Wright. The Diversity & Inclusion Council, led by Jan Harrington-Davis, weighed in at multiple pivotal points to help broaden our perspectives about how healthcare leadership needs to evolve. My colleagues in education and practice in the National Council on Administrative Fellowships have also been important sources of perspective and support. Finally, I could not possibly have written this book while still running NCHL, and I owe a debt of gratitude to LeAnn Swanson for taking over its leadership in 2020.

I am grateful to the team at Berrett-Koehler for encouraging me to pursue this book, and shape it into the contribution I hope to make to the field. Thanks especially to Leslie Iura, Edward Wade, and Kate Gibson at Westchester Publishing Services.

I finally want to thank my wife, Deborah, who gave me the encouragement and space to pursue this project, and my kids, Emily and Tyler, who gave me every reason to seek the kind of long-term progress this book seeks to support.

Index

A3 (PQI approach), 117

Accelerate (XLR8) (Kotter), 146

accountability partner, 29–30

ACHI. *See* Association for Community Health Improvement (ACHI)

action competency domains, 3, 32. *See also* execution; relations; transformational change

active listening, 89–94

Act phase of process and improvement cycle, 119

Affordable Care Act (2012), 13

Agency for Healthcare Research and Quality, 121

American College of Healthcare Executives, 69

American Hospital Association, 134

American Planning Association, 165

American Society for Healthcare Human Resource Administrations, 68–69

analysis stage, in system development life cycle (SDLC), 66

anchoring to the culture, in transformational change, 143

anchor institution concept, 14–15, 134

annual cycles: budget, 51; human resource management, 56

approval, budget and purchase, 53, 54–55

Arbery, Ahmaud, 9

artistic component, in RIASEC personality model, 87, 89

Asana, 116

Association for Community Health Improvement (ACHI), 134

Association of Change Management Professionals, 146

associations. *See* professional associations

assumptions: interpersonal understanding and, 85–86; during team leadership formation, 104

ATMs (automated teller machines), 64

attentiveness, active listening and, 91–92

attracting and recruiting, in employment life cycle, 56–57

audits, 51

automation, 63–64

autonomy, threat of organizational change related to, 144

average life expectancy, 14

Baldrige (PQI approach), 117
Becker's Hospital Review, 67–68
benefits plan changes, 56
"Best places to work" contests, 56
bias, performance measurement
    and, 112–113
board of directors, 53
board of trustees, 53
boundary-spanning, 122–134;
    community collaboration,
    131–132; formal organ-
    ization structure, 127–128;
    informal organization
    structure, 128–131; orga-
    nizational awareness,
    127–131; relationship and
    network development,
    123–126; strengthening,
    132–134
Boyatzis, Richard, 82
*Brag! How to Toot Your Own Horn
    without Blowing It*, 82
brain, self-awareness and the, 71
Brown, Brené, 82
budget cycle, 51–55
"burning platform," 139
burnout, clinician, 8, 77, 83
Burrus, Daniel, 157–158
bystanders of transformational
    change, 140–141

Calm app, 82
Carbon emissions, 19–20
Case Western Reserve University
    (CWRU), 82
CDC. *See* U.S. Centers for Disease
    Control and Prevention
Center for the Study of Ethics in
    Professions, 44

central connectors, 131
certainty, threat of organizational
    change related to, 143–144
certifications, project manage-
    ment, 120
Certified Change Management
    Professional (CCMP)
    credential, 146
chain of command, 128
champions of transformational
    change, 140, 141
change. *See* transformational
    change
change models, 137–143
chart, formal organization
    structure, 127–128
claims management, in revenue
    cycle, 49–50
claims processing, in revenue
    cycle, 49, 50
clinicians: burnout, 8, 77, 83;
    changing roles of, 10–12;
    information systems and,
    64; professional networks
    and, 125
coercive power, 95
collaborative overload, 131
comfort zone, 80–81, 142
commitment levels, from team
    members, 106
communication: active listening
    for, 89–94; among team
    members, 107–108; of
    change vision, 140
communities and community
    collaboration: anchor
    institutions and, 14–15;
    health systems' role in,
    13–14, 19–20, 131–132;

health systems' role in addressing problems in, 19–20; hospitals investing in, 15–17; mentors/role models for, 133; organizations for, 18, 133–134; "quarterback organizations" and, 19
three key approaches to, 18–19
Community Health Needs Assessment (CHNA), 13–14
community service projects, 25, 108
compensation and benefits (HR department), 59
competing values, 37–39
competitiveness of compensation, 58–59
computer-assisted tools in healthcare, 10
consolidating gains, in transformational change, 142–143
contentment, 76. *See also* well-being
conventional component, in RIASEC personality model, 87, 89
Coursera platform, 69, 82
COVID-19 pandemic, 7–8, 79
CPHQ (certified professional in health quality), 120
Crucial Conversations: Tools for Talking When the Stakes Are High (Patterson), 109
customer service metrics, 112–113
cybersecurity, 64–65
cycles: budget, 51–55; employment life cycle, 56; human resource management, 56;

process and quality improvement, 117–119; revenue cycle, 47–51; system development life cycles (SDLCs), 65–66

Dare to Lead (Brown), 82
data and data collection: CHNA/ CHIP activity, 13–14; foresight planning, 160, 165, 166–167; human resource, 60–61; information systems and, 61–67
decision-making, in teams, 107–108
departmental leaders, budget goals made by, 52–53
design stage, in system development life cycle (SDLC), 66
difficult goals, 115
direct report, 127
discretionary effort, reward power and, 96
disruptive innovation, 159
DMAIC (PQI approach), 117
Do phase of process and improvement cycle, 118–119
Dyer, Jeffrey, 109
Dyer, Jr., W. Gibb, 109
Dyer, William, 105, 109

egocentric goals, 115
electronic health records (EHRs), 62, 64–65
e-mail lists, 67–68
employee engagement surveys, 56
employee resource groups, 108
employees: COVID-19 and, 79; engaging and developing, 59–60; foresight planning and hiring of, 164–165; in

employees (*continued*)
formal structures of organizations, 127; hiring, 57–58, 164–165; hospital expenditures on, 17; job transitions, 60; leaving their positions, 60; as part of health systems, 20; salaries, 57–59, 80; wellbeing in, 78–80. *See also* healthcare professionals/professions; workplace attracting and recruiting, 56–57
employment: automation and, 63–64; laws on salary, 58; life cycle, 56–61; professional networking and gaining, 123. *See also* workplace
enabling competency domains, 32. *See also* health systems literacy; self-awareness; values
engaging and developing stage of employment life cycle, 59–60
enterprising component, in RIASEC personality model, 87, 88
environmental sustainability, 134
execution, 3, 110–121; ingredients of good, 114–115; performance measurement and, 111–114; process and quality improvement approach to, 115, 116–118; project management approach to, 115–116; relations skills and, 110; strengthening, 119–121
expectations, team members discussing individual, 106–107

expenditures/expenses: approval of, 54–55; in the budget cycle, 51, 52; community investments and, 15–16; on information systems, 62; personnel, 17, 55
expert power, 96, 129–130

fairness: salaries and, 58; threat of organizational change related to, 144–145
false consensus effect, 86
Federal Reserve Bank of San Francisco, 18
feedback, 27–29, 40; agreeing on a path forward with, 102–103; creating a safe climate for, 99; describing your expectations with, 100–101; describing your observations with, 101; ending with supportive or encouraging comments, 103; identifying a shared context for your, 99–100; risks associated with, 97–98; seeking a shared understanding with, 101–102; self-awareness and, 71–73, 80; self-confidence and, 74–75, 97; steps for designing/providing, 98–103; study on, 97
financial performance, monitoring of, 53–54
financial resources, 47–55
fiscal year, 51
Fisher, Roger, 109
flowcharting, 118
Floyd, George, 9

focus, for active listening, 89–90
foresight strategies and resources, 156–168; analysis framework, 159–164, 165, 168; data sources, 165, 166–167; hard trends and, 157–159; personal time horizon, 156–157; personas, 163–164, 168; scenarios, 163, 165; uses of, 164–165
formal structures in organizations, 127–128
forming phase of team development, 104
formulation, budget, 52
future: importance of thinking about and planning for, 155–156; signals about the, 137; strategic orientation and, 136–137. *See also* foresight strategies and resources
The Future of the Professions: How Technology Will Transform the Work of Experts (Susskind and Susskind), 44

"gaming the metrics," 112
Gates, Bill, 9
Getting to Yes: Negotiating Agreement without Giving In (Fisher and Ury), 109
Gibson, William, 137
Goals: articulating team, 107; leadership needed for, 24–25; measuring performance of, 111–114; setting good, 114–115
Goodman, Larry, 14

Google, 79–80
Griffith, John, 69
group-centered goals, 115
guesses (inferences), active listening and, 93
guiding coalition, for transformational change, 139

HAN (Healthcare Anchor Network), 134
hard trends, 157–159
Headspace app, 82
health: community collaboration's influence on, 131–132; data collection in order to improve, 13–14; relationship between quality of healthcare and, 17–18; well-being as foundation to, 76–77
healthcare: computer-assisted tools in, 10; costs, 12–13; inequalities, 7–8; inequities in, 7–8; relationship between health and quality of, 17–18
Healthcare Anchor Network (HAN), 134
Healthcare Delivery Providers (online course), 69
Healthcare Financial Management Association, 69
healthcare organizations. *See* health system(s)
healthcare professionals/ professions: addressing carbon emissions, 19–20; career-focused learning programs for, 17; power differential between patients and, 10–11, 21; trend in

healthcare professionals/
professions (*continued*)
relationship expertise of, 9–12;
value sets in, 36. *See also*
clinicians; employees; leader(s);
leadership development;
professional network(s)
Health Care Without Harm, 134
Health Information Management
Systems Society, 69
Health-Related Quality of Life
website, 83
health screenings, for human
resource management, 56
health system(s): barriers to
well-being in, 77, 79; carbon
emissions impact, 19–20;
community collaboration
and, 13–14, 19–20, 131–132;
during COVID-19 pan-
demic, 7–8; financial
resources, 46, 47–55; foresight study on, 8–9; growth
of, 12; human resource
management in, 55–61;
information systems in,
61–67; people as common
denominator in, 20–22.
See also healthcare; healthcare professionals/
professions
health systems literacy, 3, 46–69;
financial resources, 47–55;
human resource manage-
ment, 55–61; information
systems, 61–67; strengthening your, 67–69
helpers of transformational
change, 140

hierarchies in organizations, 22,
127–128, 147
hiring and onboarding, in
employment life cycle, 57–58
hiring events, 56
hiring staff, foresight planning
and, 164–165
Holland, John, 86
hospitals: cash stockpiles, 16;
cybersecurity threats to, 65;
expenditures on informa-
tion systems, 62; expenditures on personnel, 17;
infection control in, 63;
information systems and,
62; investment in communities, 15–16; Practice Greenhealth membership, 134
human population growth, 158
human resource management,
55–61

implementation: budget, 53; system
development life cycle (SDLC),
66; transformational change
phase, 140–142
industry e-mail lists, 67–68
inertia, 12, 136, 157–158
infection control in hospitals, 63
inference, active listening and, 93
influence, leadership and, 94.
See also power(s)
informal organization structure,
128–131
informational power, 96, 130
information systems, 46–47,
61–67
information technology, 129–130
innate ability, 26, 27

Inspirational Leadership through Emotional Intelligence (course), 82
Institute for Alternative Futures, 165
Institute for Healthcare Improvement, 121
Institute for the Future, 165
insurance coverage, 48, 49, 50
interpersonal understanding, 85–86
Introduction to Project Management (course), 121
investigative component, in RIASEC personality model, 87, 88
Investing in What Works for America's Communities, 18
inviting further contributions, for active listening, 91–92

job fairs, 56, 123
job prospects, networking and, 123
Johansen, Bob, 8

Koranne, Rahul, 69
Kotter, John, 137, 146
Kotter model, 137–143
Kottke, Thomas, 83

labor unions, 60
leader(s): overconfident, 74–75; overinvolved, 41; reasons for following, 25–26, 84–85; reasons for wanting to lead, 24–25; steps in becoming a, 23–24; underinvolved, 41–42
leadership and leadership role(s): being prepared for, 1; changes in, 147–148; climate change and, 19–20; cultivating well-being, 78–80; helping others develop, 97–103; power and influence in, 94–97; practice in, 26–27; team, 103–108; values in the, 39–42
leadership development, 30, 148; for boundary-spanning, 132–134; for execution, 119–121; feedback from others and, 27–29, 72–73, 80; for health systems literacy, 67–69; practice and, 26–27; reflection and, 29–30; for relations, 108–109; for self-development, 80–83; for transformational change, 145–146; values and, 42–45; for well-being, 81
Leading Change (Kotter), 138, 146
Lean (PQI approach), 117
Lean Six Sigma (PQI approach), 117
legitimized power, 95, 127
life expectancies, 14
LinkedIn, 126
listening, active, 89–94
long-term perspective. *See* foresight strategies and resources

maintenance stage, in system development life cycle (SDLC), 66–67
managers: organizational change and, 145; reporting structure and, 127; responsibility of, 127

mandatory training, for human resource management, 56
massively open online courses (MOOCs). *See* MOOCs (massively open online courses)
mastery experiences, 75
mature leadership style, 40–41
McGonigal, Jane, 137
meaning in life, 34–35
medical bills, 50
medical records (employee health records), 62, 64–65
meditation, 78, 82
meetings: with mentors, 151–153; team operating guidelines discussed at, 107, 108
mentors and role models, 43–44; approaching potential, 150–151; for boundary-spanning, 133; definition, 149; ending your relationship with, 154; first meeting with, 151–152; learning about change leadership from, 146; learning about execution from, 120; learning about health systems from, 68; learning about values/values conflict through, 43; managing your relationship with, 152–153; professional associations and, 44; reasons for mentoring, 149–150; "reverse mentoring," 108; for self-development, 81–82; strengthening relations skills through, 109

mission(s): articulating team, 107; of Google, 79–80; of health systems, 131
mission of organization, 53
mobile devices, distractions from, 90–91, 98, 101, 102–103
Modern Healthcare, 68
Monday.com, 116
MOOCs (massively open online courses), 69, 82, 121
mortality, personal values and, 34–35

National Academies of Science, Engineering, and Medicine, 83
National Center for Healthcare Leadership, 2, 8, 32, 124
network development. *See* professional network(s)
news services, strengthening health systems literacy through, 67–68
norming phase of team development, 105

objective sources, 160, 162
online courses. *See* MOOCs (massively open online courses)
open enrollment, employee benefit, 56
operating guidelines, 107–108, 117–118
organizational awareness, 123, 127–131
organizational change. *See* transformational change
organizational values, 36–37, 44–45

organizations: anchor institutions, 14; for community collaboration, 133–134; hierarchies within, 22, 127–128, 147; "quarterback," for community development, 18–19. *See also* health system(s)

overconfidence, 74–75

overinvolved leaders, 41

over-the-counter medications, 11

pandemics, prediction of, 8–9. *See also* COVID-19 pandemic

paraphrasing content, 92

past-due medical bills, 50

patient(s): as common denominator in health systems, 20–22; electronic health records (EHRs) and, 64, 65; power differential between providers and, 10–11, 21; revenue cycle and, 48, 49, 50

patient satisfaction measures, 113–114

Patterson, Kerry, 109

peer sharing, 124

people analytics, 60–61

performance appraisals, for human resource management, 56

performance measurement, 111–114

performing stage of team development, 105

personal values, 34–35, 37–38

personal values matrix, 44

personas, 163–164, 168

personnel expenditures, hospital, 17

PESTLE category set, for analysis framework, 160

physicians. *See* clinicians

Piper Alpha oil rig explosion (1988), 138–139

planning and monitoring, HR departments' focus on, 60–61

planning stage, in system development life cycle (SDLC), 66

Plan phase of process and improvement cycle, 117–118

PMP (project management professional) certification, 120

population growth, 158

power(s), 94–97; coercive, 95; defined in leadership context, 94; expert, 96, 129–130; information, 96, 130; legitimized, 95, 127; referent, 96–97; reward, 95–96

"power by job description" (legitimized power), 95, 127

practice: for leadership development, 26–27; self-confidence and, 73–74

Practice Greenhealth, 134

pre-authorization stage of revenue cycle, 49

preparation for practice, 26, 29, 73

process and quality improvement (PQI), 116–119, 120, 121, 135

professional associations: asking mentors and role models about, 44; building your network through, 125; learning about human resources, 68–69; learning

professional associations (*continued*)
about professional values
through, 43; protecting
professional status of
clinicians, 10–11
professional network(s): benefits
of, 123–124; building your,
125–126; online presence
and, 126; peer sharing
through, 123–124
professional values, 35–36, 38–39,
43, 44, 132–133
project management approach,
115–116, 120, 121
project Management Institute, 120
project timeline, 116
protocolizing, 63
psychological response, 75–76
purchases, approval of, 54–55

quarterback organizations, 19
quarters, in budget cycle, 51–52

ransomware, 65
realistic component, in RIASEC
personality model, 87–88
referent power, 96–97
reflecting the implications, for
active listening, 93
reflecting underlying emotions,
for active listening, 93
reflection and reflective practices:
feedback and, 29, 73; for
mentoring relationship, 153;
well-being and, 78, 79
regression toward the mean, 114
relatedness, threat of organizational change related
to, 144

relations, 84–109; having others
believe in you and, 84–85;
interpersonal understanding
and, 85–86; personality/
individual differences and,
86–89; power and, 94–97;
providing feedback and,
97–103; strengthening,
108–109; in team leadership,
103–108
relationships. *See* boundary-
spanning; mentors and role
models; relations
reporting, in budget cycle, 51–52
reporting structure, as element of
formal structure, 127
research (health system), 9–10
resisters of transformational
change, 141–142
resources for learning, 30; about
boundary-spanning, 133–134;
about change leadership,
146; about execution, 121;
about foresight planning,
165–168; about health
systems literacy, 68–69;
about relations skills, 109;
about self-development,
82–83; about values, 44–45
revenue: in budget cycle, 51, 52;
hospital, for community
health, 15
revenue cycle, 47–51
reverse mentoring, 108
reward power, 95–96
RIASEC personality model, 86–89
Rock, David, 143
role models. *See* mentors and role
models

"root cause analysis," 118
round robin method, 106–107
Rush University Medical Center, 14

salaries, 57–59, 80
SCARF model, 143–145
scenarios, 163, 165
Schwartz, Shalom, 44
self-advocacy, strengthening
    your, 82
self-awareness, 70–73, 91
self-confidence, 73–76; building,
    75–76; developing your,
    80–81; feedback and, 74–75,
    97; resources about, 82; role
    in leadership, 73–74
self-deceptions, 70–71
self-development, 3, 70–83;
    strengthening, 80–83
self role, imbalances between
    leadership role and, 41–42
sensemaking, 143–144
sense of urgency, for transforma-
    tional change, 139
service documentation, in revenue
    cycle, 49
short-term wins, in transforma-
    tional change process,
    141–142
signals, of changes, 137
Six Sigma (PQI approach), 117
smartphones, distractions caused
    by, 90–91
social component, in RIASEC
    personality model, 87–88
social determinants of health
    (SOD), 18
social modeling, 75
social network analysis, 131

social persuasion, 75
social support/relations: profes-
    sional network, 123–124;
    well-being and, 78
*The Social Transformation of American
    Medicine* (Starr), 69
Society for Human Resource
    Management, 68–69
software: budget approval for, 54, 55;
    for project management, 116
span of control, 128
specificity, goals possessing, 115
staff groupings, as element of
    formal structures, 127
staff retention, 60–61
Starr, Paul, 69
status, threat of organizational
    change related to, 143
STEEP category set, for analysis
    framework, 160
storming phase of team develop-
    ment, 104–105
strategic orientation, 136–137
student interns, 108
Study phase of process and
    improvement cycle, 119
subjective sources, 160
subjective well-being, 76–77
suspending judgment, 91
suspending judgment, active
    listening and, 91
Susskind, Daniel, 44
Susskind, Richard, 44
system development life cycle
    (SDLC), 65–66

*Taking Action against Clinician
    Burnout*, 83
talent acquisition, 56–57

talent insights, 60–61

Team Building: Proven Strategies for Improving Team Performance (Dyer, Jr., Dyer, and Dyer), 108

team leadership, 103–108, 109

technology(ies): automation, 63–64; changing role of healthcare professions and, 9–12; electronic health records (EHRs), 62, 64–65; expert power and, 129–130; mobile devices, 90–91

telehealth, 10

ties in healthcare and, 7–8

time commitment, measuring team members', 106

time horizon, 156–157

timeline, project, 116

top-down leadership, 22

Total Quality Improvement (PQI approach), 117

total rewards (HR department), 59

Toyota Production System (PQI approach), 117

trade-offs, among values, 37–38

transformational change, 135–146; change leadership, 137–140; implementation of, 140–142; preparing for, 138–140; strategic organization and, 136–137; strengthening, 145–147; sustaining, 142–143; threats related to, 143–145; understanding threats and opportunities of, 143–145

transitioning stage of employment life cycle, 60

Tuckman, Bruce, 104

underinvolved leaders, 41–42

union stewards, 60

University of Adelaide, 121

Ury, William, 109

Usability.gov website, 168

U.S. Centers for Disease Control and Prevention, 76, 83

U.S. Department of Health and Human Services, 121

U.S. Department of Labor, 86

values, 3, 33–45; competing, 37–39; conflicts, 39, 43; explained, 33; interpersonal understanding and, 85; in the leadership role, 39–42; organizational, 36–37, 44–45; personal, 34–35; professional, 35–36, 132–133; strengthening and learning about, 42–45

vision development, for transformational change, 139

volunteering: for community health, 132; learning about transformational change through, 145; practicing process and quality improvement through, 119–120; in professional associations, 125–126; strengthening relations sills through, 108

volunteers, definition of health systems including, 20

well-being: community, 13, 19; cultivating in others, 78–79; definition, 76; as foundational to good health, 76–77;

improving within health systems, 77, 79; leadership development and, 81; learning more about, 83; managing, 78; self-development and your personal, 82; in the workplace, 79–80, 81

"Well-Being in All Policies" (Kottke), 83

The Well-Managed Healthcare Organization (White and Griffith), 69

White, Kenneth, 69

work activities, as element to formal structures, 127

workforce planning, 60–61

workplace: benefits of active listening in the, 93–94; feeling listened to in the, 93–94; impact on health outcomes, 21–22; well-being and, 79–80, 81. *See also* employees; employment

World Economic Forum, 165, 168

World Health Organization, 76

About the Author

Andrew N. Garman, PsyD, is professor in the Department of Health Systems Management at Rush University in Chicago and director of the Rush Center for Health System Leadership. He previously served for nine years as CEO of the nonprofit National Center for Healthcare Leadership, where he remains involved in an advisory capacity. He has published over 100 research articles, book chapters, and major reports on leadership and foresight topics, as well as four books, including *The Future of Healthcare and Exceptional Leadership*. Garman received his PsyD in clinical psychology from the College of William & Mary, his MS in human resource development from the Illinois Institute of Technology, and his BS in psychology with a mathematics concentration from Pennsylvania State University.

Dear reader,

Thank you for picking up this book and welcome to the worldwide BK community! You're joining a special group of people who have come together to create positive change in their lives, organizations, and communities.

What's BK all about?

Our mission is to connect people and ideas to create a world that works for all.

Why? Our communities, organizations, and lives get bogged down by old paradigms of self-interest, exclusion, hierarchy, and privilege. But we believe that can change. That's why we seek the leading experts on these challenges—and share their actionable ideas with you.

A welcome gift

To help you get started, we'd like to offer you a **free copy** of one of our bestselling ebooks:

www.bkconnection.com/welcome

When you claim your **free ebook**, you'll also be subscribed to our blog.

Our freshest insights

Access the best new tools and ideas for leaders at all levels on our blog at ideas.bkconnection.com.

Sincerely,

Your friends at Berrett-Koehler

Certified

Corporation